DATE DUE

DEMCO 38-296

THE ROOTS OF WESTERN CIVILIZATION

a

leyden

r

Illustration Research and Captions: An Delva

Executive Illustration Editor: Paulien Retèl

Historical File Editors: Mario Damen, Piet Lekkerkerk

In Focus Editor: Nordwin Alberts, Audiovisuals & Fotografie, Almere, the Netherlands

Window-author: Art Jonkers

Art Director: Henk Oostenrijk, Studio 87, Utrecht, the Netherlands

Assistant to the Executive Editor
Hannellieke Haasbroek

Assistants to the Executive Illustration Editor
Mirjam Cornelis
Harry Jongerius

Production coordination
Elisabeth de Ligt
Henk van der Zee, Graphic Partners, Haarlem, the Netherlands

Typesetting
Libertas Pre-Press Service, Utrecht, the Netherlands

Lithography
Reprocolor Llovet, Barcelona, Spain

Printing
Mohndruck Graphische Betriebe GmbH, Gütersloh, Germany

Drawings, maps, pictograms
Euromap Ltd., Pangbourne, Great Britain
PS Holland, Amsterdam, the Netherlands
Reprocolor Llovet, Barcelona, Spain
Studio 4D, 's-Hertogenbosch, the Netherlands

Translation of chapters into English
Language Solution, Amsterdam, the Netherlands
Babel, Utrecht, the Netherlands

Translation Historical File and captions into English
Babel, Utrecht, the Netherlands
Marc van Dommelen, Terneuzen, the Netherlands

Cover: A. von Menzer, 'Suits of armour', 1866.
Greek vase painting, 6th century BC.
The ruins of the Alcazar in Toledo.

First American Edition. Edited and updated by Grolier Educational Corporation, 1994.
© HD Communication Consultants BV, Hilversum, the Netherlands, 1993.

ISBN 0-7172-7336-9
Set B&M: 0-7172-7324-5
Cataloging information may be obtained directly from Grolier Educational Corporation.

THE ROOTS OF WESTERN CIVILIZATION

TWO THOUSAND YEARS OF WARFARE

11

Editorial Board

 Grolier Educational Corporation
SHERMAN, TURNPIKE, DANBURY, CONNECTICUT 06816

TWO THOUSAND YEARS OF WARFARE

Palamedes Palamedesz., 'The army camp', early 17th century.

CONTENTS

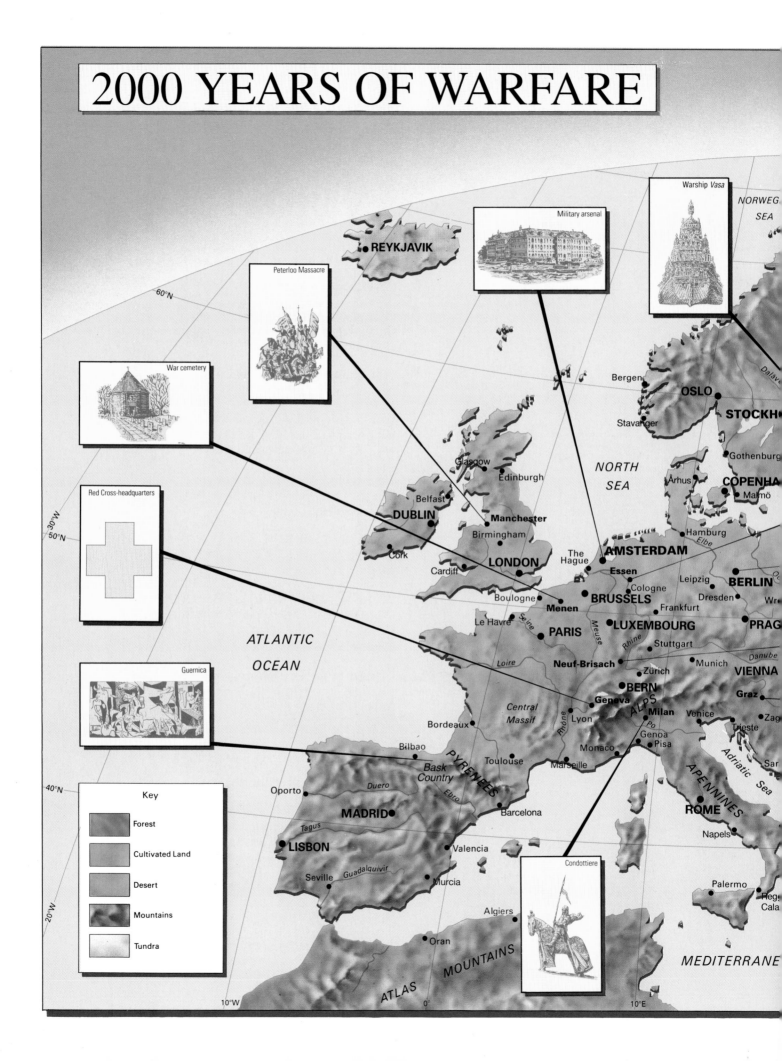

2000 YEARS OF WARFARE

War cemetery

Peterloo Massacre

Military arsenal

Warship *Vasa*

Red Cross-headquarters

Guernica

Condottiere

NORWEG
SEA

REYKJAVIK

60°N

Bergen

OSLO

STOCKH

Stavanger

Gothenburg

NORTH
SEA

Glasgow

Edinburgh

Århus

COPENHA

Malmö

Belfast

DUBLIN   Manchester

Birmingham

Hamburg
Elbe

Cork

LONDON   The
Hague   AMSTERDAM

Cardiff   Essen   Leipzig   BERLIN

Boulogne   Cologne

Menen   BRUSSELS   Dresden   Wr

Le Havre   Frankfurt

Seine   PARIS   Meuse   LUXEMBOURG   PRAG

Rhine   Stuttgart

30°W

50°N

ATLANTIC

OCEAN

Loire   Neuf-Brisach   Munich   Danube

Zürich   VIENNA

BERN

Central
Massif   Lyon   Geneva   ALPS   Milan   Venice   Zag

Bordeaux   Rhône   Po   Genoa Trieste

Monaco   Pisa   Adriatic

Bilbao   Sea   Sar

Bask   Toulouse   Marseille

Country PYRENEES   APENNINES

40°N   Duero   Ebro

Oporto

MADRID

ROME

Barcelona

Tagus

LISBON

Napels

Valencia

20°W

Seville   Guadalquivir

Murcia   Palermo

Algiers   Reg
Cala

Oran   MEDITERRANE

ATLAS
MOUNTAINS

MOUNTAINS

10°W   0°   10°E

Key

Forest

Cultivated Land

Desert

Mountains

Tundra

Barents Sea

Murmansk

White Sea

Arkhangel

N. Dvina

18th century galleons

Tank

Ob

Irtysh

Gulf of Bothnia

HELSINKI

St. Petersburg

Perm

Chelyebinsk

Peace demonstration

Volga

Riga

Gorki

Kazan

Dvina

MOSCOW

Fortification by Vauban

dańsk

Minsk

Volga

Ural

WARSAW

Pripet

Don

stula

Kiev

Kharkov

Volgograd

Dnieper

Aral
Sea

CARPATHIANS

Dnepropetrovsk

Rostov

Landeszeughaus

Prut

Odessa

Sea of
Azov

UDAPEST

Crimea

CAUCASUS MTS.

CASPIAN
SEA

BUCHAREST

LGRADE

Danube

BLACK   SEA

BALKAN MTS.

Varna

Tbilisi

Baku

Skopje

SOFIA

Araxes

TIRANA

Istanbul

Pindus

ANKARA

Kizil

Phalanx

Florence Nightingale

Kayseri

Tigris

ATHENS

Izmir

TAURUS MTS.

Euphrates

Scale 1:16,000 000 approx

SEA

NICOSIA

| 0 km | 200 | 400 | 600 |

| 0 miles | 200 | 400 |

20°E

30°E

40°E

50°E

Preface

The entire history of Europe has been shaped by the forces of war. Throughout human existence – and not only in these last two thousand years of European history – communities have settled their problems and disputes by force as well as by peaceful consensus. In the sixth century BC the Greek philosopher Heraclitus called war 'father of all and king of all', while to the eighteenth century English philosopher Hobbes war was the natural condition of mankind, a kind of law of nature, a merciless struggle 'of every man against every man', from which humanity could only break free with the greatest difficulty, by creating legal sanctions and controls.

The dramatic, powerful and continuing history of war has left an indelible mark on European history, erasing and re-drawing the political contours of Europe, and at the same time shaping its economic and social development and intervening dramatically in countless aspects of its daily life. It is no accident that other volumes of *The Making of Europe* make such frequent reference to war, or that even the volume devoted to 'Forces of Faith' includes themes (such as the crusades or the wars of religion) that are unmistakably part of the history of war.

In the present volume, however, war is not merely a counterpoint or background to the wider history of Europe. Instead, we have attempted to reconstruct a history of war 'from within' – a history of military formations, of the ways in which battles were actually fought, of the weapons and equipment used, of warfare, tactics and strategy, at various significant moments that serve to underscore the main trends. In discussing the ancient world, we will focus on the main features of warfare in the scattered, advanced Greek *poleis*, and on the huge military machine that the Romans created in order to establish and preserve their empire. In our discussion of the medieval world, when societies were built on war as an all-pervading, commonplace feature of their social fabric, the central theme will be the rise of chivalry (with all its social and political implications) and its subsequent fall owing to the far-reaching changes in warfare that took place between the end of the Middle Ages and the start of the modern era. In the world of the Renaissance and the Ancien Régime, we will look at two mainstays of warfare: fortresses, which, besides being major instruments of war, were to become lasting features of the European urban and rural landscape, and shipyards, offstage reminders of the appalling, cruel spectacle of naval warfare. Shortly afterwards, with the French Revolution, the nature of warfare was to change yet again, owing to the introduction of weapons of mass destruction (coupled with immense loss of life on the battlefield) and the emergence of a 'war industry': the mass production of weapons and military equipment, with ever more sophisticated and destructive techniques that ultimately cancelled one another out. The tragic patterns of frontier warfare, with its immense tactical deployments and its highly developed instruments of war, reveal the enormous price paid on both sides in terms of human lives reduced to utter worthlessness.

Inevitably, however, the various essays continually refer to more general topics. War has remained closely linked with the economy (through the impact of wartime destruction – another recurring theme of horror, from the sackings and burnings of the Middle Ages to the mass bombardments of our own era – and in recent decades its close involvement with industry, finance and the arms trade), with the history of attitudes (the rise of nationalism and ideology as ways of rallying the population) and with daily life and ways of thinking.

Another theme that cuts across the history of war concerns the link between war and the political organization of society. In particular, war is closely linked to the origins of the 'modern state': the huge resources involved in warfare ensured that it became a monopoly of the state, and thus an increasingly telling and decisive factor in overall state policy. The increasing interdependence of modern nations meant that wars, hitherto fought between individual states, became 'international' – in other words, they were henceforth fought between opposing groups of allied states. These opposing alliances and alignments were to have a decisive impact on the overall make-up of what came to be known as the European powers, and they became the principal mechanism in an increasingly inflexible power structure. Even within individual states, the growth of the military apparatus led to stricter, more rigid internal controls in the form of greater coercion, especially in the monarchies of the early modern era. One result of this increased capacity for oppression was that even conflicts with internal opposition movements automatically turned into open warfare. This happened in various European countries between the sixteenth and eighteenth centuries, and more recently in the Spanish Civil War, which can also be seen as an example of the intrusion of ideologies into local conflicts, of overt or covert foreign intervention: a type of warfare which in recent decades has recurred frequently in various parts of the world, including Europe.

Giorgio Chittolini
Supervising Editor

Skeletons engaged in a ghastly bayonet fight: a variation on the medieval theme of the *danse macabre*, painted by Anton Romako in 1885.

Two thousand years of warfare

In two millennia the role of war has undergone substantial changes.
The main concern of the late Roman Empire was to maintain a defense force to protect its borders. In the Middle Ages war was perhaps the most important instrument for enabling internal exploitation. War was both an economic and social necessity for the ruling classes.
In the long term, while wars have become fewer in number, they have become increasingly destructive.

Jan Lindegren

Greek warrior on horseback, a bronze statuette probably made in Taranto (southern Italy), c. 550 BC.

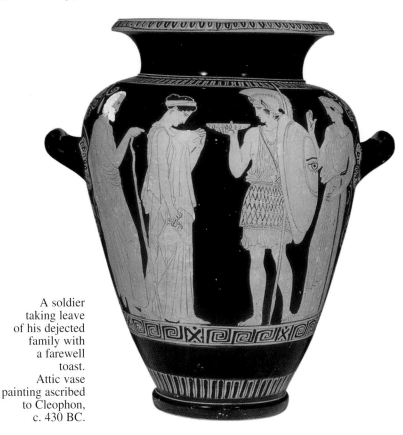

A soldier taking leave of his dejected family with a farewell toast. Attic vase painting ascribed to Cleophon, c. 430 BC.

From Pax Romana to European wars

From the days of the Roman Empire until our own era war has been an ever-present threat, part of everyday life. Throughout this period war in some form or other has been going on continuously in Europe. In fact it is war which has largely formed the Europe we now know. Practically all the present European states have borders which were determined by war. What is more, the states were to a large extent formed by wars. It may reasonably be maintained that most of the present European states, and practically all their defunct precursors, were once built up as organizations for waging war.

Two thousand years ago *Pax Romana* prevailed: blessed peace. It came to be regarded by scholars as an ideal condition. However, the Roman peace was hardly peace in the modern sense. War was waged on the borders of the Roman Empire and even within, in the form of rebellions and conflicts between political factions, piracy, banditry, etc. Large contingents of soldiers were kept to maintain the Pax. Estimates range from 400,000 to 600,000 men, equivalent to 1% of the population of the Empire.

This considerable military strength ultimately proved inadequate in repelling wave upon wave of Germanic invasions, despite the fact that the Romans had far greater military resources than the Germanic tribes. It must be said that the Empire had largely collapsed from within, with repercussions for the armed forces which were only capable of mobilizing about a quarter of their manpower. What remained was reorganized into the Eastern Roman or Byzantine Empire.

With the fall of the Roman Empire the ability to wage war on a large scale disappeared for a very long time. War became localized, regional conflicts waged by smaller forces or more often plain armed bands. The Germanic tribes invaded the Roman Empire bent on plunder. For them war was a form of exploitation, in contrast to the late Roman Empire and the Byzantine Empire, where the armed forces had developed into expensive defense mechanisms. To begin with, the Germanic tribes were engaged in external exploitation, just like the Vikings in later times. Gradually, however, they established themselves as part of society and turned into feudal barons. War was still central to all exploitation, but it was now fought out between different feudal barons. This does not mean that the art of war had not developed. The medieval knights were far more formidable warriors than the foot soldiers and horsemen of Roman times. On the other hand they were incapable of organizing large-scale wars because of the fragmentation of power. By the late Middle Ages, however, this fragmentation of power was stemmed and a new centralization took place.

Before this came about, however, organization was strictly along feudal lines. The overlord, the king or emperor, or equivalent not only had his subordinate territorial vassals, who in turn had their vassals, and so on, but he often had a relatively large number of direct vassals like royal abbots for example who could probably provide twenty or thirty knights each to serve their overlord. Every knight was in turn provid-

The battle of Actium (31 BC), in which Augustus defeated his rival Marc Antony, was a watershed in Roman history, and caused the suicide of the Egyptian queen Cleopatra. 18th century painting of this event by Johann Georg Platzer. On the middle galley Marc Antony is depicted, while Cleopatra can be seen on the ship at the right.

ed with a number of armed assistants. In addition foot soldiers of different kinds were brought in, which meant that the knights only constituted a minority in the armies.

In principle the vassal system gave access to a large number of knights. It has been calculated that there may have been as many as 35,000 in Charlemagne's empire. However, neither he nor his successors were in any position to mobilize all of them; including all the other soldiers, there must have been more than 100,000 men. Eventually it became increasingly difficult to persuade the vassals to go to war. This was mainly because the rights and obligations of the vassals were being defined within increasingly restricted territorial boundaries. As a result war service came to be limited both in time and space. The vassals maintained, with growing success, that their compulsory service covered only the defense of the duchy, bishopric or county, and then only for short periods of time. These limitations in compulsory service meant that the overlords were forced to pay for the vassals' services when they had to use them on a large scale. This development is epitomized by the position taken by the knights of Champagne in 1315. They claimed that they were only obliged to answer the king's call within their own county, and then only if they were paid wages by him. Against that background it is not sur-

Replica of an Anglo-Saxon helmet (7th century) with visor, found in the excavation of the burial ship of Sutton Hoo.

Medieval footmen, armed with spear, sword and shield, listening to the admonitions of their commander, clad in a coat of mail and helmet. Detail of a miniature, c. 1200.

English archer drawing an arbalest. Such bows shot heavy bolts, often bearded arrows, over great distances. Margin miniature from the 'Book of Hours' of Sir Luttrell (c. 1335).

the knights and then to maintain their skill, was even more expensive. The wages paid them during the campaigns of war, which were often very limited in time, were small by comparison.

The increasingly prohibitive cost of training and equipping knights spawned a cheaper variant of the heavy cavalry: the *sergeants*. These were trained in the same way as the knights, except that their equipment was simpler and they had fewer horses. Although their lower social rank and humbler origins set them apart from the knights, the *sergeants* were still part of the upper stratum of society. The heavy cavalry was also supplemented with other soldiers, both mounted and on foot. Like knights and *sergeants*, these were often highly qualified military experts such as crossbowmen and archers. It is interesting to note that these groups were also recruited from more wealthy strata of the population. In the Middle Ages the obligation to keep weapons was in principle determined on the basis of wealth and was restricted to freemen.

The formation of states and other bodies capable of waging large-scale wars benefitted in some respects from the crusades. With the crusades some important changes were introduced. Firstly, the wars were fought against an external enemy, and secondly, a special form of tax was sanctioned for financing the crusades. In short an extra tax for fighting foreigners was invented.

However, the random nature of the crusades was insufficient to support permanent centralized structures. Similarly there was a need for access to continuous exploitation for the purpose of building up major state-controlled armed forces. To achieve these things, both the possibility for exploitation and an almost constant war against an outside enemy had to exist. Both these conditions were fulfilled in France during the Hundred Years' War. The fall in feudal rents in the late Middle Ages created room for exploitation and this was achieved by imposing war taxes on the population. These taxes were justified by the continuing war against England.

Even before this came about the English and French kings in particular had succeeded in gathering together huge armies, mainly by substantial increases in the number of foot soldiers. What they were unable to do, however, was to keep these armies intact for more than a few weeks. The problems of pay and supplies quickly became acute and could not be solved within the framework of the existing exploitation system. But to assemble the armies at all required highly developed administrative skill, and this is where the writing desk really came into its own in planning wars.

The population catastrophe resulting from the spread of the Black Death across Europe in the mid-fourteenth century also had major effects on the history of war and its development quite apart from the reduction, in terms of numbers, in the size of armies in the following century. As a result of the reduction in the population feudal rents declined, and competition between feudal landowners for peasants meant that no

prising that it became the rule to pay even in cases where compulsory service could be enforced in principle. Such compulsory service was increasingly replaced by a tax which was used to pay the warriors' wages.

Although the extent to which war service could be demanded of the vassals was ever decreasing, the system was kept intact because it was essential to have access to the heavily armed, well-trained knights. The cost of keeping oneself in armor and horses was very high, but the accompanying lifestyle, including hunts and tournaments, which was at first necessary to train

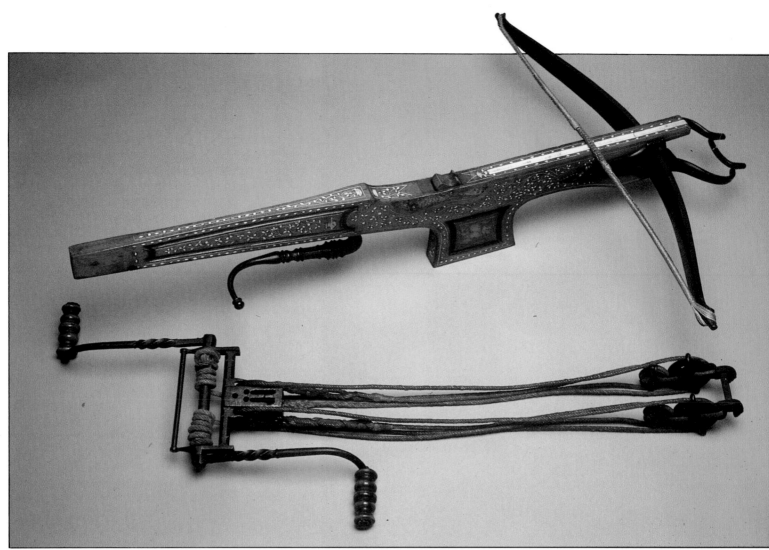

Crossbow from Limoges (16th century) with mother-of-pearl tessellation. Beside it the matching winding reel to draw the string.
Crossbow archers were always deployed behind longbow archers in the attack formation, since they needed more room to keep the bow in level position, as well as more time to draw the bow.

one could unilaterally extract more from his subordinates. It was in this very situation that royal taxation for war purposes was developed. The continuing war legitimized the taxation, and because it was coordinated the ruling class was able to further its position at the expense of the peasants. This meant that war, with its attendant taxation apparatus, eventually became increasingly important for the redistribution of the societal surplus. Previously the ruling class had lived largely off what could be extracted in various ways from the subordinate peasantry and to a certain extent from what profits might be made from the beginnings of trading in goods through tolls, the right to mint coins and similar arrangements. The size of their own domain was the most important factor in deciding both wealth and power. And war was about enlarging this area at the expense of others. The situation was the same when the kings went to war with each other or with their vassals. Now the armed forces, the organization of war, the court, became an important means of redistributing wealth. At the same time war came to be almost a vital necessity for the princes. Without war they would not have been able to control the redistribution of the surplus, and then their power would have been greatly limited. Without war the prince would also have been unable to monopolize the

On August 8, 1342, the English (at the left) and the French fought an inconclusive battle off the coast of Brittany. This contemporary miniature shows an attempt to board enemy ships; the ensuing man-to-man combat was usually fought with bows, spears and axes.

Three steel daggers, two of which with richly ornamented scabbards, all made in Switzerland in the last quarter of the 16th century. The dagger was a multi-functional, fearsome weapon, which could effortlessly pierce a coat of mail, or cut the straps of a helmet.

right to use 'social force', a right which was obviously guaranteed by the existence of strong, permanent armed forces.

War and the European state system

The development of standing armed forces can of course be said to be partly the result of an almost permanent state of war. But it can also be ascribed to a conscious political strategy, which was undoubtedly aimed at strengthening the power of the prince. During the final phase of the Hundred Years' War the French King Charles VII (1422-1461), and perhaps to an even greater degree his son Louis XI (1461-1483), took the unprecedented step of organizing a major army on a permanent basis, an army which was not disbanded when peace eventually came. Worse still, Louis expanded these forces, much to the regret of his contemporary chronicler who commented that the many thousands of soldiers still collected five francs a month even though they were quite peacefully allowed to stay at home. However, the king was not happy with the French soldiers and acquired in addition six to eight thousand Swiss foot soldiers from Germany, who were paid year in year out despite remaining at home – no one could remember them taking part in any war.

Other princes were forced to follow the French example. During the last quarter of the fifteenth century a permanent force of 20-25,000 men was maintained in France. By its very nature it was a different kind of force than the medieval army of knights. By then the German *Landesknecht* and the Swiss foot soldiers had replaced the knights and when Charles the Rash, Duke of Burgundy, was defeated by the Swiss at Grandson and Morat (1476), and finally at Nancy (1477), where he himself fell in battle, the supremacy of the foot soldiers had begun.

In fact it could be said that Louis XI had the dubious

Even in his lifetime the military genius and commander Francesco Sforza was likened to the great generals of antiquity. This flattering 15th century fresco by Giampietrino shows him engaged in conversation with Fabius, Scipio, Pompaeus, Julius Caesar, Hannibal, Epaminondas and Themistocles.

Erasmo da Narni (1370-1442), nicknamed *Gattamelata* ('honeysweet cat'), was a reliable *condottiere*, well versed in the theory of warfare. In 1424 he served Florence, from 1432 he was hired by the Vatican. In 1434 the pope seconded him to the Venetian Republic, and in 1439 he assisted Francesco Sforza in his feud with the Viscontis of Milan. Donatello (1386-1466) perpetuated his image in this magnificent equestrian statue.

honor of creating modern Europe in that he succeeded in building up the first permanent massed army. Pressure from France meant that surrounding areas were forced to organize themselves similarly in one way or another. This did not necessarily take place within the framework of the dynastic state, for a long time it was possible to secure the continued existence of apparently insignificant principalities with the aid of various coalitions and associations. At the same time it is clear that the new nation-states would come to dominate the international scene. Or it could be said, perhaps, that they made up the scene, which was Europe, and the drama played out was international war. It was against this background that Niccolo Machiavelli maintained that 'a prince therefore should have no other object or thought, not regard anything as much his business, as the art of war and its institutions and discipline. For that art is the only one expected of a ruler'.

Princes of this particular kind soon became legion, and it was they who created the Europe as it has since become by maintaining international relations, the core of which was war. However, this development cannot be entirely attributed to the pressure which

Swiss women and children being abducted, while their male relatives are helplessly looking on. Victorious commanders usually let their troops sack conquered cities; they would plunder the civilian population, not only men, but also women, who were often raped during the pillaging, or abducted, only to be raped later. Swiss miniature from 1485.

'The Lumley Horseman' (c. 1580), a life-size iron-shod statue made of polychromed wood, is the oldest known English equestrian statue. The horseman, dressed in a typical Renaissance harness with tunic, is wielding an axe. The horse is wearing head protection with a projecting jag.

France brought to bear on its neighbors, and they in turn on their neighbors. Obvious internal pressure to change the forms of exploitation was quite general. The Black Death and the fall in income from estates in the late Middle Ages were general phenomena, but in Eastern Europe the feudal lords were successful in overcoming these difficulties by limiting the competition for peasants by means of the so-called second serfdom. As a consequence of this institutional solution taxes were not required to promote the position of the feudal nobility. However, where attempts to tie the peasants more closely to the land were unsuccessful and peasant freedom grew, the situation was roughly the same as in France. But there was also another country which exerted roughly the same amount of pressure on its neighbors in Northern and Northeastern Europe as France, and that was Sweden.

There is every reason to examine Sweden's role in the creation of the European state system because it is relatively unknown to most people. During the period 1560-1719 Sweden was involved in a large number of wars. The years of peace were few – only a quarter of that period – and during the remaining 120 years the country was involved in 1.6 wars per year. Up until 1660 a highly expansionist policy was pursued, a policy which on the whole was so successful that one region after another came under Swedish domination. The policy of war that was pursued also resulted in continuous increases in the level of exploitation in the country up till around 1620. After that date it was impossible to extract more from the peasants. At the same time the apparatus and costs of war were growing and eventually led to an ever harder struggle for resources among different social elites. Increasingly larger groups of society's upper strata were losing more on the war than they were gaining. Slowly but surely support for the war policy eroded. But war, and the financing of war, soon took over from the internal distribution policy. After the death of Gustav II Adolf (1632) it was clear that Sweden could no longer extricate itself from the war being waged at that time, even though there was a desire to do so among the leading factions. The war financing system was based largely on future payments, and peace would have involved very high costs which could not be met if the war did

In 1507 King Louis XII of France rode through the vanquished city of Genoa at the head of a triumphal procession. He wore a plumed helmet and had four prominent inhabitants of Genoa carry his royal baldachin. In the foreground girls are begging for mercy; bystanders are looking on impassively.

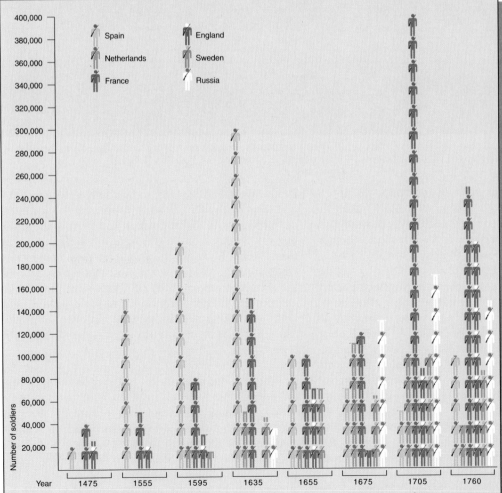

In the bloody battle of
Marignano (Lombardy, 1515) the
victorious French artillery inflicted
heavy losses on its Swiss
opponents, supported by Maximilian
Sforza and Pope Leo X. Some
20,000 troops lost their lives in
this encounter, which lasted
for two days. In the foreground, at
right, King François I of France
is depicted on horseback,
leading his cavalry into battle.
Drawing by the Master
of *La Ratière*.

The size of the armed forces
of some powerful European nations
between 1475 and 1760.
England only started to build up a
large standing army in the
18th century, at a time when
Spain and the Netherlands were
already past their prime.

Legend:
- Spain
- Netherlands
- France
- England
- Sweden
- Russia

Y-axis: Number of soldiers
400,000 / 380,000 / 360,000 / 340,000 / 320,000 / 300,000 / 280,000 / 260,000 / 240,000 / 220,000 / 200,000 / 180,000 / 160,000 / 140,000 / 120,000 / 100,000 / 80,000 / 60,000 / 40,000 / 20,000

X-axis: Year — 1475, 1555, 1595, 1635, 1655, 1675, 1705, 1760

J. Tintoretto painted a cycle of eight historical paintings for the Gonzaga family in their Mantua palace, portraying heroic feats from the lives of these margraves. This is the impressive assault and capture of Parma in 1521 under the command of Frederick II Gonzaga.

not result in territorial gains. In addition to this it was extremely difficult to discharge mercenary troops for there was of course the risk that a hostile power might take them into its service. It was therefore thought better and safer to allow the war to continue as long as it was waged in Germany.

The Swedish wars were waged mainly against Eastern powers. Russia, Poland and Brandenburg/Prussia all lay within the area of the second serfdom. For all intents and purposes the boundary between Eastern and Western Europe followed the Elbe. In some respects Denmark might also be classified as an Eastern country, for there had been some success, on the Zealand group of islands, in tying the peasants to the estates by means of the so-called *vornedskabet*, the purpose of which was to prohibit the male population from moving from their place of birth. Internal pressure to reorganize the state on the basis of taxation was therefore weak in all these states. But under the influence of pressure from Sweden, Denmark and

Brandenburg/Prussia were to be completely converted and eventually Russia was modernized. However, developments in Poland, which had to bear the main brunt of Swedish onslaught, went in a different direction. From a historical viewpoint the developments in Denmark and Poland are the most interesting. During the sixteenth century both countries were prosperous and powerful. Both were major regional powers, and both were subjected to extreme pressure from the ascending power of Sweden during the seventeenth century.

In Denmark the property-owning nobility did its best for a long time to block royal attempts to build up a strong standing army. But they eventually gave in when Sweden proceeded to conquer the entire country at the end of the 1650s. Royal absolutism was introduced in 1660, quickly leading to an enormous redistribution of social resources from the nobility to the crown, and by using these resources a very strong army and an adequate administrative apparatus were built up. It is interesting to compare developments in Denmark with those in Poland. On the brink of the disaster the king of Denmark succeeded in dramatically strengthening the princely power and subsequently organizing a modern European state. However, the resources available to the Danish crown were considerable even before the introduction of absolutism. It has been estimated that during the seventeenth century the central government could dispose of about a quarter of the surplus production. After the change of system in 1660 this rose to approximately 55%. In Poland the initial position was different because the royal household had far fewer resources, relatively speaking. But the Polish feudal state was both very large and very rich in relation to its northern and western neighbors and for a long time these resources were sufficient to fend off attacks successfully. Some decades into the seventeenth century, however, it became quite clear that the Polish army was completely out of date. Later the attempts to reform the army were inadequate. From the point of view of the magnates it happened to be more advantageous to seek to retain the agricultural surplus for themselves rather than relinquish substantial means to build up a strong central power capable of chasing off foreign invaders. When it turned out that they were invading the country with frightening regularity, Poland sought to solve its problems by choosing as king in 1697 the Saxon elector, August the Strong, whose state had a significant, modern army. But not even this afforded complete protection. Yet there is every indication that the fate of the Polish aristocratic republic should not be regarded as a disaster either for the elite of the country or for its population as a whole. The elite probably gained economically by not giving in to a centralized power as their Danish counterparts did, and being subject to a military state of the Swedish, Danish (from the 1660s and beyond) or Prussian model was certainly not desirable.

The price of war

To some extent war in early modern Europe also imposed new demands on the princes. One of the most important was expressed by Marshall Gian-Jacopo

The battle of Pavia dealt France a serious blow, which even involved the capture of King François I by the Habsburg army. Two of his sons were taken to Madrid as prisoners in the monarch's stead; they were released – for an exorbitant ransom – only after the peace of Cambrai in 1529. Tapestry from the series 'The Battle of Pavia', woven after the designs by Barend van Orley.

The distribution of herring and white bread among the emaciated population of Leyden after the prolonged Spanish siege was broken on October 3, 1574. Painting by Otto van Veen.

Emperor Charles V inspecting his troops near Barcelona before embarkation on an expedition to Tunis (1535), where they inflicted a heavy defeat on the Turks. Tapestry made in 1712-1721, woven after a design by Jan Cornelisz. Vermeyen, who witnessed the event in person. In the 18th century the Austrian emperor Charles VI still prided himself on this feat to support the Habsburg propaganda.

Silver scale model of a 16th century hulk with guns, made by Hans Schlottheim. This ship, serving as a table clockwork, was part of the famous collection of Emperor Rudolph II in Prague.

become even more monetarized. To meet the almost inexhaustible demand for money, most areas succeeded in taxing their own populations. However, the war taxes were wholly inadequate, which is why they were supplemented with loans on future incomes. To eke out their coffers most of the princes employed the method of devaluation. When credit had reached rock bottom, which happened almost everywhere, there were no options left but state bankruptcies. Spain holds the record, with eight state bankruptcies between 1557 and 1698. But the demand 'money, money and more money' also conceals a different reality. Most of what was produced in the society of the sixteenth and seventeenth centuries, and to an even greater degree in the Middle Ages, was food which went for more or less immediate consumption, without giving rise to any appreciable market relationships.

Of course there were exceptions. Even during the Middle Ages some regions were well on their way towards a market economy. The successful uprising against Spanish rule in the Netherlands during the sixteenth century and the exceptionally powerful position of the Dutch state for most of the seventeenth century was dependent on the enormous economic potential of the area at that time.

Apart from Holland, and later England, however, most major states were struggling with a serious problem. The states and the princes needed mainly an internationally negotiable currency used largely for conversion on the war market, while production was aimed at subsistence. In order to figure on the international stage access to means of payment, silver and gold, were required. States did not just wage war against each other with armed forces, but they also fought an unrelenting, constant economic battle.

Money was needed to acquire soldiers and provide

Trivulzio in 1499 when he explained to the French king Louis XII what was needed for the impending campaign in Italy. The Lombard commander declared that he needed 'money, money and more money'. This had always been the case, of course, but now war had

An ambushed army convoy is attacked by warriors coming out of the woods. Such attacks were often a means of obtaining weapons, ammunition and food from the enemy. Painting by Paulus van Hillegaert, early 17th century.

them with weapons and clothes, to keep them in the necessities of life, to pay them wages, to establish fortifications and to build and equip warships. With the rapid increase in the size of armies, these needs also grew fast. Technical development, in the form of better weapons, rendered medieval fortifications obsolete. New, extremely expensive structures had to be built.

The need for soldiers was dictated both by the size of armies and by the losses they had to sustain. There is a great deal of information available on the size of armies, although it is often vague. The size of some of the more important European armies during the period up until the French Revolution is indicated in a separate table.

The trend is clear. Three centuries after Louis XI began to build up the standing French army the phenomenon had become generalized and the forces were twice as large. Together with England and Spain, France maintained about 85,000 men around 1475. In 1760 these three powers had a combined strength of around 550,000 men. At the same time the population in the three countries had grown from about 30 million to 45 million, which means that the proportion of the soldiers of the population had increased from about 3 per thousand to 12.

Most humble, Admiral Justin of Nassau hands over the keys to the city of Breda to his Spanish opponent, Admiral Ambrosio Spinola in 1625. 'The Surrender of Breda', better known as *Las Lanzas*, is a masterpiece by Diego Rodriguez da Silva y Velazquez.

21

To assess the recruiting requirement, however, the size of the losses must be realized. How dangerous was it for soldiers to go to war? The general picture is both of scarred veterans surviving for decade after decade and masses of soldiers dying on the battlefields. War losses tend to have been equated with deaths in pitched battles. Yet this was not so in this period. Ordinary soldiers rarely died in battle. Far more often they succumbed to diseases which resulted from the hardships of a soldier's life. Poor diet and at times lack of food, worn clothing and a shortage of accommodation threatened their health.

During all the wars waged by Sweden in the period 1620-1719 a total of 500,000 native Swedes and Finns died. About 10% of them were killed in battle or died of wounds. A further 10% did not survive being taken prisoner of war. The remaining 80% died of diseases. It was therefore far more likely for soldiers to die during the everyday experience of war than actually in battle. There is no reason at all to suppose that conditions in the Swedish armies differed very much from those of other countries.

On average the soldiers survived for three to four years, i.e. 25-30% of the forces had to be re-recruited annually, apart from the replacement of deserters and soldiers sent home for one reason or another. In the particular case of Sweden, whose armies almost without exception fought outside its own boundaries where the local population spoke a language which the soldiers did not understand, desertions were not a serious problem. Only a few were foolhardy enough to escape the army in a foreign country. The heading 'deserters and those killed by peasants', which is often seen in Swedish source material from the days of the Thirty Years' War, says it all. However, the situation was completely different if the war was being fought on or in the immediate vicinity of one's own territory. Then desertions were a very serious military problem.

Poor soldiers

But let us return to fatalities. Because it was the everyday reality of war which claimed the overwhelming majority of all victims, the number of dead may be regarded largely as a function of how long the soldiers were mobilized and how many of them there were. One of the most significant differences between the waging of war in the Middle Ages and in the early modern period was that the latter was characterized by the fact that the states and princes were able to keep large masses of troops gathered for months and years at a time, whereas in the past it had been only possible to keep major armies assembled for a matter of weeks. It is probably for that very reason that they were not affected by the mass death which afterwards became the trademark of war.

The proportion of Swedes in the army was very high compared with the population throughout the seventeenth century, 3-4% of the population, much higher than the figures given above for Spain, France and England. It should be noted, however, that the Spanish army was on a par with the Swedish army in terms of size, around the year 1635. Later the ranks were not filled in, which obviously lightened the recruitment burden. During the period 1620-1719 a total of 30% of all Swedish and Finnish men who survived childhood died during active service. A further 10% had also fought in one war or another, but survived. Statistically a 15-year-old male could expect to live another 40 1/2 years in the mid-eighteenth century. Women of the same age lived for another 43 years. During the seventeenth century, however, 15-year-old boys could

Johan van Oldenbarneveldt's private army handing over its weapons in Utrecht in 1618. On May 13, 1619, Van Oldenbarneveldt was executed for high treason and deliberately disturbing the religious, ecclesiastical and political relations in the Dutch Republic.
Painting by P. van Hillegaert, 1627.

In the middle of the 16th century the pistol was introduced in the cavalry. This is a detail of an encounter with handheld guns and rifles, which Palamedes Palamedesz., called Stevaerts, painted before 1638.

The Swedish war industry was developed with Dutch assistance. During the second half of the 17th century Sweden became one of the main European heavy weapons producers. This is a cannon foundry at Julitabroeck, painted by Allaert van Everdingen.

only count on living another 32 years, while girls could expect to live another 44 years. War had made Sweden a country of women and children. The situation of women in particular had changed. Because of the high losses there were two single women to every single man. This meant that a much higher proportion of women in the population than before and after this period did not marry. This in turn led to a situation where far fewer children were born than at any other time.

How was it possible for society to tolerate losses of this size for a century or more? This brings us straight to some of the most central problems in understanding war and the waging of war in the seventeenth century. The princes of early modern Europe were well aware of the disadvantages of mass armies. For one thing new ones had to be kicked up at all too regular intervals, which of course was both expensive and threatened to lead to shortage of labor. All contemporaries were convinced that there was a shortage of people, a

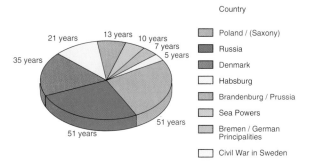

Country
- Poland / (Saxony)
- Russia
- Denmark
- Habsburg
- Brandenburg / Prussia
- Sea Powers
- Bremen / German Principalities
- Civil War in Sweden

In the 17th century Sweden became a very active belligerent nation that was almost constantly at war with one or more rival powers. Therefore, Sweden had a great many enemies between 1560 and 1719. Since the country was sometimes involved in several different wars at the same time, the total number of war years in this period of 159 years was 193. The neighboring countries, Poland, Russia and Denmark, suffered most due to the Swedish expansion.

23

it would be a good deed to relieve the country of these imagined masses and send them off to the army.

The problem was that this line of reasoning was unrealistic. There was certainly a large proportion of the population among European peasant societies which could not feed itself completely. But in most cases this meant the sick, the handicapped or the old who were not suitable as soldiers. The proportion of thieves and tramps was small. Moreover, where these did exist they generally knew how to evade the recruiters. The larger the towns and cities the more advanced the economic life, the more numerous were these layers of the population. Paris was therefore one of the most important recruiting areas for the French army. In England this category of population was sufficiently large to ensure a major proportion of the recruitment into the armed forces. Germans and Scandinavians found their way into the Netherlands and could also be recruited. But in most places there was a shortage of suitable soldiering material, and even in England, France and the Netherlands their own *Lumpenproletariat* was far from sufficient.

In this situation it was possible to engage in foreign enlistment, as Louis XI had already done, in order to avoid burdening one's own labor force. This meant that someone else's labor force was obviously burdened. Who, then, went into the massed armies of the new era, apart from the poor of the large cities? To a substantial extent it was people from the various war areas, people who for one reason or another gave up the peasant life there and instead joined one of the armies, which, of course, was a rational choice in view of the recurring devastation that war brought. The typical soldier, however, had an entirely different background.

He came from one of Europe's marginal agricultural areas. First there were the Swiss Alpine valleys, then the Scottish Highlands which supplied warriors, followed thereafter by other similar areas. They all had one thing in common. Agriculture in those areas was unproductive, and only small plots of land were cultivated. Moreover, the soil was light to till. The rearing of cattle and other secondary activities were of vital importance to sustaining life. In such areas the peasants produced only an insignificant surplus, which could be extracted from them in the form of rent or taxes. The loss of male labor was not a problem because the men did not produce more than they consumed. Even more important, however, was the fact that in practice there was no particularly sharp division of labor between the sexes – women could do most of the work men did when they were at home.

This was not the case on the great clay plains. There the men were needed for any agriculture to be practiced. If there was insufficient male labor when the

Talks between two high-ranking officers in the French army.
Wash drawing, c. 1690.

notion which sprang naturally from their intellectual and physical roots in the recurring epidemics and the agrarian crises of the late Middle Ages. In their view peasants and other producers should not in principle be recruited into the new armies. Instead one should try to take the riff-raff, the non-supporting but only consuming pack of humanity that was thought to drift around the country causing all sorts of trouble. In fact

The splendid Royal Navy Hospital (1694) on the northern bank of the Thames at Greenwich was built for war invalids and elderly soldiers and paid for by the state. Its architect was Christopher Wren. Greenwich Hospital continued to be used until 1896; in 1873 the admiralty had taken over the building. Painting by Canaletto.

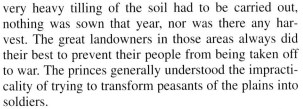

very heavy tilling of the soil had to be carried out, nothing was sown that year, nor was there any harvest. The great landowners in those areas always did their best to prevent their people from being taken off to war. The princes generally understood the impracticality of trying to transform peasants of the plains into soldiers.

A very large proportion of all soldiers was therefore recruited from the marginalized agricultural regions of Europe. These soldiers were cheap to acquire and they could be had in almost unlimited numbers without rendering the domestic economic situation precarious. This situation was utilized by clan chiefs in the Scottish Highlands, the Luneburg dukes, who lived on hiring out regiments, and others, among them the

The 'musketeers' were French elite troops armed with muskets. They were given harsh military training with numerous drill exercises; witness this medal from 1665, which belonged to Thomas Bernard.

Swedish seventeenth century regents who perhaps did so on the most grandiose scale of all. Women in most of marginalized Europe coped fairly well, at least in an economic sense, even though there was a shortage of men. And because of this the princes could recruit excellent soldiers who were used to living in harsh conditions.

At the end of the 18th century coke replaced charcoal as the main fuel for iron smelters. The development of puddling furnaces, in which air was added to the hot iron mass, led to the manufacture of high-quality steel, to the benefit of the war industry.

The proclamation of the French Republic (1792) brought about a social revolution in the French army, when tens of thousands of citizens volunteered for service. Foreign mercenaries, who until then had dominated the armed forces, were replaced by a popular army of peasants and *sans-culottes*. For them patriotism meant a break with their traditional bonds. Detail of 'Napoleon on the battlefield of Eylau, 1807', a painting by Antoine-Jean Gros.

After 1789, 800 French healthy young men were quickly trained as gunners, to defend the young revolution. Here a gunner in training, en route to an exercise.

Rich battlefields

Of necessity, however, wars had to be waged in the large, rich agricultural regions. Expressed in simple terms it may be stated that wars were fought on the large plains by poor people from the slowly growing large cities, and particularly by people from forest and mountain regions. By methods organized by various princes these men found their way down into the rich agricultural areas and were used at the expense of the resident peasants. Some of the latter grew tired of feeding the inhabitants of the forests, mountains and cities and instead joined them, allowing their former brothers to continue feeding them. It could not have been otherwise.

If a map of modern Europe is viewed from this perspective it is all quite striking. Wars were really fought in the very best agricultural areas. Countless battles were fought in Flanders, which was for a long time perhaps the very best agricultural region of all. Austrians and Frenchmen regularly went to Italy to do battle on the Po plain. The Swedes fought their wars in rich Denmark or went to Poland, which was one of Europe's foremost granaries in the seventeenth century. Russians and Brandenburgers/Prussians also went to Poland. One of the causes of Poland's hardships was that it constituted the most important arena of war for its neighboring powers. However, Polish agriculture

was highly inefficient compared with that of the Flemish, and this had easily discernable, though hitherto overlooked, consequences for how wars were conducted.

In Flanders there was a sevenfold return on sowing in the sixteenth century, and a nine- or tenfold return in the seventeenth century. In Poland there was a fourfold return. The military significance of this was simple: six or even more times as many soldiers – if allowance is made for the higher degree of cultivation – could remain in a west European war zone of the same area as an east European one. In turn the rich agriculture made it possible to build large, strong and above all tightly packed fortifications, which was not

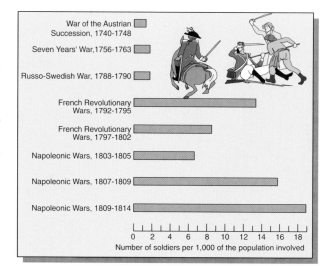

From the last quarter of the 18th century onwards, great changes took place in the ways of warfare. The armies became larger, which was due to the fact that new forms of government came into being, especially after the French Revolution: the people made their entry in politics and became more and more involved in warfare because of mass mobilization and military service. Because of these phenomena, Napoleon was able to raise large armies.

possible in Poland, where the installations were sparsely distributed.

As a result of this the west European war took a completely different shape to the east European war. In Flanders very large armies could be assembled in the region, lying almost still to monitor each other. The most important thing was to capture each other's fortifications. In Poland, on the other hand, the armies had to move around constantly in the hunt for food. The war was therefore much more mobile and the armies consumed what food and fodder was available very quickly. Obviously different types of cavalry units played a greater role in Poland than in Western Europe simply because the ability to cross large areas quickly was so important.

Despite these differences warfare in this period was dictated by the same considerations in both areas. The main objective of all military operations was to provide one's own troops with the best possible upkeep and, if possible, to outmaneuver the enemy and prevent him from supplying himself. Purely military and political objectives of various kinds were of secondary and tertiary consideration because of the necessity of surviving from day to day.

Food for the soldiers and fodder for the horses therefore constituted the hub around which warfare centered. Almost all the food and all the fodder had, of necessity, to be obtained locally within the war zone. The transport of food over long distances was unthinkable, as was the transport of fodder. During perhaps one of the best organized of the war campaigns of the seventeenth century – the French attack on the Netherlands in 1672 – the French war minister Louvois succeeded in covering 11% of the army's requirements via long-distance transport, which was considered to be unique. On some occasions major transport operations could be carried out by sea, but ashore it was necessary for food and fodder to be available within a radius of 12,5 miles from a tightly packed army. The animal feed was almost always consumed

Swiss countrymen signing up for the Berne Militia (18th century). Over the ages the Swiss have built up a reputation of a people of daunting warriors, which sent its sons abroad to serve as mercenaries. The Swiss papal guard is a remnant of this tradition. Colored drawing by Franz Niklaus König.

first. Horses eat roughly ten times as much as people per day, and in a normal army there were two horses to every three soldiers. An acute shortage of feed quickly developed, particularly when the armies were concentrated in anticipation of a field battle.

A number of methods were used to satisfy these requirements. Of course the best thing was to be able to pay one's way in ready cash, in gold and silver. As long as the army behaved in a fairly civilized manner and did the right thing problems with wilful or rebellious peasants were avoided. It was therefore a militarily sound policy to pay well for the maintenance of

This Baroque building in Berlin, with a cornice richly decorated with sculptures, was designed by a group of architects which included Andreas Schlüter. It was a weapons arsenal of the Prussian army from 1730 until 1880 when it became an army museum. Since World War II it has housed the East German *Geschichtemuseum* (history museum).

In 1814 Goya painted the popular rising of May 2, 1808, on the *Puerta del Sol* in Madrid to commemorate the Spanish resistance against the occupation of the country by the 'Tyrant of Europe', i.e. France.

methods became increasingly disorganized with devastating consequences for most of Germany. The reason was that forces that were too large were moving for too long around an area of which the agriculture was insufficient to sustain them. The shortage of food and other requirements meant that harsher and harsher methods had to be used against the peasant population, which was subjected to terrible outrages. This in turn led to progressive destruction, which soon worsened the general conditions.

Military commanders, however, generally had a clear understanding of how much a region could withstand, in terms of the amount of food extracted, without being devastated. It became almost a doctrine that armies had no right to extract more from a region than was paid under peaceful conditions in the form of tax and duties to the landowners. On one occasion Louis XIV even ordered repayment because one of his armies had levied and collected more than this norm in a foreign territory. Often, however, there were military reasons for destroying a village or a part of a country, for example to prevent an enemy force from advancing. When this was the case civil considerations - as usual - were sacrificed on the altar of military rationality.

From the Europe of war to that of peace?
The last 200 years

During the eighteenth century the nature of war gradually changed. In many places war had played out its role as an instrument for internal exploitation. The level of exploitation was as high as it could be and in this situation war was expensive in all respects. Continued economic development also had major consequences. Capitalism was creating new social classes but also better weapons of war. What was even more important was that capitalism brought about an infinitely superior production capacity compared to that of the old feudal society.

The new social classes had a different attitude to war. Previously war had been one of the most important mechanisms for redistributing the surplus in society. The old feudal nobility had passed from a warring nobility to one of office holders. But almost all earnings were more or less dependent on war. The majority were officers, but there were also a large number of civil administrators who were required to organize society in such a way that it was capable of waging large-scale wars. The capitalists, on the other hand, were interested in earning money by producing and selling goods. For them wars were perhaps a lucrative market for fortunately nothing else. Unlike their predecessors on the highest rungs of the social ladder the capitalists were not generally dependent on war, even though certain groups still were.

As has been mentioned, these changes began to make themselves strongly felt in the eighteenth century. An expression of this can be found in the noticeable reversal of attitude which took place in Scandinavia. In Sweden the role of the state was remarkably redefined from being an organization for the protection of

the army. However, the coffers of most of the warring states were too empty for armies to survive by this method, save in exceptional cases, which is why more heavy-handed methods were resorted to. The contribution method applied by Wallenstein and Gustav II Adolf was a natural one to adopt. By threatening devastation, fire and murder more or less openly, money was extorted from a region and could then be used to pay for the upkeep of the soldiers. But often even this did not work. During the Thirty Years' War such

British soldiers in London's Chelsea Hospital, injured in battle, are told the news of Napoleon's defeat at Waterloo in 1815.
One of the patients is reading aloud the newspaper report from the 'Gazette'; others give comment. Music, drinks and happy faces all evoke
the joy of the moment in this painting by Sir David Wilkie, 1822.

its subjects – waging war – to one for the development of industries. In Denmark pretty much the same happened. The political objective was peaceful development.

Conscript armies

The major, decisive change obviously came, however, with the French Revolution. First and foremost subjects were converted to citizens. As far as war was concerned this meant a transition from standing armies to conscript armies. The gigantic French armies of Napoleon's time could ignore old teachings because of their very size. A fortification of 5-10,000 men strong posed no threat whatever to armies of millions. They simply went round it and ignored it. For the first time field battles were decisive events of war due to the fact that troop strengths were now sufficiently large to occupy even large countries. The consequence of this was that all countries were forced sooner or later to conform to the French model. Soon the majority of all men in Europe were trained for war.

The conversion from subject to citizen also meant that the nation, *la patrie*, played a much more important ideological role which would be used for purposes of war. It should be mentioned that this was far from new. It is seen even in the Middle Ages. But the nationalism of the nineteenth and twentieth centuries provided, and unfortunately is still providing, far

This relic bust of the unifier of Italy, Garibaldi, shows him in the middle of an altar surrounded by bayonets instead of candles. Below the altar ex votos of the cities already liberated by Garibaldi: Marsala, Palermo, Naples, Rome and Venice. Caricature printed by D. Salvi in Milan, 1863.

Soldiers killed in combat, houses destroyed by fire and complete destruction in the neighborhood around the Saint-Privat graveyard are illustrative of the horrors of the French-Prussian war of 1871. Painting by Alphonse de Neuville.

Henri Pille's personal account of soup and bread distribution during the siege of Paris and the Commune during the winter of 1870-1871. Concentrated meat extract, an invention of the German chemist Liebig, was one of the few staples available in sufficient quantities to replace rare meat.

greater possibilities of ideologically motivated war than its forerunners.

To return to the nineteenth century: after the end of the Napoleonic Wars a new Europe emerged. It was definitely more peaceful than before, that is, wars were not waged internationally on the scale seen since the end of the fifteenth century. While wars still took place in Europe, they were largely pursued in other parts of the world by the most powerful European states who did their best to divide the rest of the world between themselves. This was certainly not done by peaceful means.

All this can be illustrated on the basis of the war history of Great Britain. After 1815 the country was only involved in one European international war up until World War I, and that was the Crimean War (1853-1856). Globally, however, Great Britain was on average engaged in 1.8 wars annually during this period. The distribution of all these war years among the different categories is illuminating to say the least. If both 1815 and 1914 are included, international European wars accounted for only three per cent of British warfare, in terms of time. Non-European colonial attempts at conquest, together with resistance movements against such attempts, took up 75% of all this time. To describe the nineteenth century as peaceful against this background is merely an expression of Eurocentered cynicism.

Obviously many of these wars were fought on a small scale from the British point of view, just as the corresponding campaigns that were waged by the other European powers from their point of view. But this was hardly the case viewed from the non-European horizon. Towards the end of the nineteenth century most of the world was divided between the major powers, and British wars tended to be fewer in number. At the same time, however, and as a result of competition among the imperialist powers for the colonies, major preparations for the coming great European war had already begun. Immediately after the turn of the century it was generally expected that war would come. Everyone knew that it was unavoidable. The question was when. Morocco? Sarajevo!

In some respects World War I represented a new kind of warfare - the industrialized war. With the aid of railways and trucks it was possible to arrange the long-distance maintenance of armies of millions. For the first time it was a much larger transport problem to bring forward weapons and ammunition than food. War was now being waged on an almost undreamed of scale. Together, conscript armies, efficient industrialized production and the possibility of long-distance maintenance created the conditions for a war of peoples. Ideologically preparations had been made for this through citizens' rights and nationalism. Around the turn of the century almost everything was thrown into the ideological battle. In France, for example, the Battle of Bovines in 1214 was made a symbol for the ancient struggle of the French against the Germans. Similar phenomena can be found in abundance everywhere in Europe. In Sweden the warrior king Charles XII was called under the banners in this time of danger. Hand in hand with this, poets and others began to maintain that war was a form of culture, the highest of all. Men ought to be cleansed by iron, fire and blood. Much of this nonsense was directed inward and used as a weapon against the emerging working class. It was this class which morally tarnished the nations and it was naturally this class which ought first and foremost to be cleansed. And so they were.

But it was not only workers and others who died in the trenches of Flanders. Fortunately most of this ideological rubbish died with them. War was no longer heroic, only dirty. But not quite. In the ideological world of Nazism and Fascism the glorification of war and violence lived on. Just before World War I such ideas were commonplace and shared by conservatives throughout the whole of Europe.

World War I might still be regarded as a logical consequence of a political development, a result of political and economic tensions in the European state system. To this extent it was an old-fashioned war which had similarities with those which broke out at the end of the fifteenth century. This was hardly the case with World War II. Now it was a question of a new world order which was to replace old, antiquated ideals. Nazism and Fascism demanded room to create the new man. Ideologically they competed with the Communist concept of a world revolution, the obvious aim of which was also to create a new man and a new world order. War was undoubtedly an integral part of the Nazi ideology.

To some extent World War II, or rather the armament

This wash pen drawing from 1903 by the Austrian artist Alfred Kubin is a sharp allegorical denunciation of war.

Wounded soldiers being taken to a field hospital during the trench war of 1914-1918. Painting by Sir Stanley Spencer in 1919.

On June 6, 1944, D day, allied forces landed on the coast of Normandy. Two days later the bridgehead with England was established, sealing the fate of Nazi Germany.

Oskar Kokoschka's painting 'Alice in Wonderland' (1942) which refers to the Austrian *Anschluss* to Nazi Germany, is pervaded with scorn and mockery.

crises resulting from too high a production capacity. Fortunately this is hardly the case.

In World War I new weapons technology finally broke through. The last memories of the medieval knights were effectively mown down by machine guns. Tanks, planes and other advanced weapons were introduced, as were the first weapons of mass destruction - the war gases. This inheritance has certainly been continued. The rapid development in weaponry which followed rendered all the theories of World War I obsolete in World War II. And so it has gone on.

The political and ideological confrontation of the Cold War between two different economic systems, two power blocks, took place, among other things, in the form of an arms race. It soon led to a situation where all human life could be blotted out several times over in just a few moments. THE BOMB has become a reality for everyone and has also had a major ideological influence on a number of different levels. But similar threats, which also portend the end of mankind, have emerged. Every day the end appears to be approaching inexorably. Recent political developments have raised the prospect that it is environmental disaster rather than bombs which threatens the future of the world, even though wars have returned to Europe.

On the last two millennia and the future

In the very long perspective the role of war has undergone substantial changes. The late Roman Empire was concerned mainly to maintain a defense power to protect its borders against invasion by the barbarians. When a new society was built on the ruins of the empire the role of the army was essentially redefined. War was perhaps the most important instrument for maintaining internal exploitation; it was no longer basically harmful but a social necessity, a way of life. With the dawn of the early modern period there was another change. The international war was now established. This was needed both to intensify exploitation and as a means of redistributing the surplus. War was therefore both an economic and social necessity for the ruling classes. Capitalism has brought about another radical change. In the long term while wars have become fewer in number, they have become increasingly destructive because the resources that can be used for warfare have snowballed. But war is no longer a dominating economic or social necessity. Instead war is political and ideological.

No one can say that the present role of war will be the same in the future. Many believe that global injustices will lead to a new kind of war motivated by economic and distribution policy between north and south. This much is absolutely clear, however: Europe has survived and has been created largely out of two millennia of war. The world will in all probability not survive another two, and for its part *Pax Romana* should have had its substitute in *Pax Mundiala* far earlier.

which preceded it, may be seen as an attempt to find a political solution to the problems of the industrialized world which sprang from the deep depression of the 1930s. There is no doubt that the build-up of arms resulted in a boost for the economies of the world. It must be added that the prolonged boom after World War II was favored by the terrible global arms race. A fairly widely accepted idea extending from these observations is that capitalism needs war to overcome

Ceramic vase in the shape of the helmeted head of a Greek warrior, dating from the 6th century BC.

War in the Greek and Roman world

War was in the Greek and Roman world a normal state of affairs.
Rules and regulations applied, if at all, to warfare with culturally 'equal'
opponents, hardly with 'barbarians'. War made possible some technical
progress and was the ultimate cause of most slavery and of the success of
Greek and Roman civilization. Eventually warfare led to a unified
and internally more or less peaceful world around the Mediterranean in
the shape of the Roman Empire.

Henk Singor

This *stèlè*
(tombstone) was
erected in
memory of Aristion
(6th century BC).
The *hoplite*, spear in hand,
is wearing a cuirass
which offers extra
protection to shoulders
and breast.
Below the waist,
the cuirass ends in strips.
A pleated tunic, woven
out of fine wool,
is worn under the thorax.
Metal greaves protect
the legs, and a simple
helmet covers
the head.

Greeks and Persians fighting in the battle at the Granikos in northwestern Anatolia.
Marble relief from the so-called Alexander sarcophagus (late 4th century BC).

One force above all determined the course of Greek and Roman history: war. There was nearly always war somewhere. It was a part of nature questioned only by a few philosophers. Only gradually did peace become a norm to the extent that war had to be started upon by an official declaration. But even so, such declarations of war were considered necessary only in dealing with one's neighbors or with states that were on an equal or comparable level of civilization. The true outsiders, the barbarians, could be dealt with without any legal or moral restraints and thus exterminated or enslaved – or subjugated and ultimately Hellenized or Romanized.

The effects of war were many. In a technologically nearly stagnant civilization it was war that stimulated some technical progress. The foundation of Greek and later of Roman colonies amidst barbarian populations was due to military superiority. The phenomenon of slavery could not have become as widespread as it did without the captives brought in by victorious armies. Greco-Roman civilization itself, being typically urban, could not have spread as it did, had it not been by force. So it was warfare that culminated into a united and only then internally peaceful world around the Mediterranean in which that civilization could penetrate the countryside and at last Romanize large parts of continental Europe.

Aristocratic fighters

Traditionally a man's social and political status was linked closely to his ability to fight. To a large extent, this explains aristocratic supremacy in early Greece and Rome since only the elite had horses and metal armor at their disposal. Then, in the classical period of the fifth and fourth centuries BC, the citizen militia largely dominated the battlefields. In politics, it was the age of democratic or moderately oligarchic regimes. The appearance of the professional soldier and the mercenary in the course of the fourth century BC made possible the great territorial states based on conquests that characterized the age of Alexander and his Hellenistic successors. These as well as the conquests of the Roman Republic made the city-states and the citizen-armies obsolete, requiring standing armies and permanent commanders-in-chief. Thus the great Hellenistic monarchies and finally the Roman Empire arose with its professional legions and its *imperator* as sole head of state ruling a disarmed population of citizens and subjects.

It has been stated that the contribution of Greece to the history of warfare consisted of the introduction of new battle tactics in the form of the line formation of heavy infantry fighting in close order with short-distance weapons like spears and swords aimed at crushing its opponents by the sheer shock and weight of its organized mass. But this is surely an overstatement. Not only did warfare in ancient Greece often differ from this model, but the line formation itself cannot be regarded as a Greek invention. What the Greeks did, though, was stiffen that line and develop its tactics to near perfection, thereby fashioning the shape of battle for more than 1,000 years. The *phalanx*, as the line of heavy infantry was known in Greece, made its first appearance in history at around 700 BC in the verses of Homer. It was made up of the best fighters, either fighting in very small companies on their own, or acting as a thin screen in front of a mass of lesser-armed people. In both cases, only small numbers were involved. The tactics themselves can be interpreted as a special development of the champion role aristocratic fighters had to perform in ancient times.

In the seventh and sixth centuries BC, however, foreign contacts generally brought more wealth for the elites of the Greek city-states and enabled them to monopolize the military function of the state to a large extent. More and more, the lower classes, who could not afford to equip themselves with bronze armor, tended to be excluded from the battlefield. So the Archaic Age was the heyday of aristocratic warfare. The bronze-clad warriors fought in close ranks and armies that consisted of a few hundred men at the most. The larger populace was called up to fight, with whatever they might have, only in times of emergency, like when the existence of the community was at stake. As a rule archaic warfare was rather restrained. Wars were seldom fought to the finish and were often characterized by certain restrictions (like a ban on long-distance weapons, avoidance of destruction of vital goods or areas, an obligation not to attack the opponent unawares etc.). All this applied only to Greeks, however (and even then was not always observed), and not to war between Greeks and barbarians.

The statue of this Greek hero, shown in heroic nakedness and ready for combat (5th century BC), formed part of the front freeze of the *Aphaea* temple on the island of Aegina. This Doric temple was probably built during the Persian wars.

15th century miniature depicting the tale of the Trojan horse.
According to this tale the huge wooden horse, which the Greeks had left behind on the shore before setting sail, was wheeled into the city by the guileless Trojans. During the night the Greek warriors came out of the hollow horse, took the city and destroyed it by fire.

In archaic and classical times only members of the aristocracy could afford a horse to ride in battle. This splendid mural painting, showing a Campanian cavalryman with shield, was made c. 370 BC and was found in a tomb in the Greek colony of Paestum, south of Naples.

Citizen-soldiers

Although the Greek *phalanx* originated in an aristocratic world, it was in a different environment that it

This is the famous scene from Homer's *Iliad*, in which fleet-footed Achilles carries the body of Hector, his opponent, from the battlefield. Detail of a painted vase, 6th century BC.

acquired its historical significance. Probably because of intensifying competition between the city-states (with some of them, notably Sparta, enabled by their special internal organization to put many more heavily armed men in the field than others), most Greek cities enlarged their armies in the latter half of the sixth century. Hand in hand with this development, and indeed often as its precondition, body armor became lighter and cheaper. As a result, in the fifth century BC Greek heavy infantry used only bronze shields for protection. Helmets, cuirasses and greaves were no longer invariably of metal but usually made of leather, felt, or linen for the rank and file. Roughly half of the free population could equip themselves in this manner as *hoplites*, as these citizen-soldiers were now normally called.

The hoplite armies of classical Greece were much larger than those of the preceding age. The main cities like Athens, Argos or Thebes could raise armies of up to 12,000, 7,000 or 6,000, respectively. Sparta, also drawing on non-citizen troops from its territory, could put some 6,000 men in the field. Yet land warfare kept many of its 'aristocratic' traits. Ambushes and surprise attacks were frowned upon. The decisive battle took place as a bloody tournament in a well-known and open space. Captives were as a rule returned for a ransom and the dead handed over for proper burial. Above all, tactics other than those of the hoplite *phalanx* were virtually disregarded well into the fifth century. This meant that cavalry remained underdeveloped and that light-armed skirmishers with javelins, slings or bows hardly played any role, while fortification almost always held the better of a still rudimentary siege technique. In social and political terms it meant that the lower classes of the population, because of their lack of military value, could not exert any political influence. The hoplites could, of course, and many aristocracies in Greece had their base broadened to absorb these 'middle classes'. Only in Athens could the poorer citizens exercise a military role as rowers of the war fleet, itself a creation of the early fifth century and the wars against the Persians. This certainly is part of the explanation for classical democracy in Athens.

The old rules and norms of archaic and aristocratic warfare lived on to some extent in a sort of unwritten code of 'Hellenic laws' applying to warfare between the Greek city-states. Much of that code was broken, but it did provide a certain standard and was to some extent a forerunner of modern international law. In practice, though, hoplite warfare was a rough and bloody affair. Devastation of crops and orchards usually accompanied a campaign. The battle itself was a deadly encounter of nervous amateur soldiers running headlong into each other with rows of spears outstretched. Casualty rates of 5-10% for the victors were normal, and generals and officers in the front line ran a special risk. The fallen numbered at least twice as many on the side of the defeated. Only the Spartans were disciplined professionals who preferred to march steadily where the opponents ran and to sing their old war songs where the other side yelled in excitement or panic. But they could afford to take the time for military exercises, having a large serf population to do their daily work. In a certain sense, the Spartans continued the practices of the archaic age, both in war and in other areas. Real innovation was not to be expected from these conservative professionals. This came from the amateurs of the other cities.

Professionalism

After the Persian Wars (490 and 480/79 BC), the victorious Greeks had taken up their internal competitions again, and the city of Athens was, thanks to its fleet and to its hoplites, able to assemble a whole league of cities de facto submitted to it. The ensuing struggle between Athens and its 'alliance' against most cities of mainland Greece under the leadership of Sparta in the Peloponnesian War (431-404 BC) ushered in a new phase of warfare that was finally to destroy the independence of the cities themselves. The bitterness of the struggle gave rise to new tactics and new techniques. Foremost the light-armed troops reappeared on the stage, and with them the ambush and the ruse of war. Cavalry became more important. Siege warfare developed and the first use of siege engines was perfected in the next century. Above all, professionalism spread. The last years of the fifth century witnessed the rise of the mercenary soldier:

View of the Peloponnesian city of Mycenae. On top of the small hill lies the fortress of the Mycenaean kings, which is over 3,000 years old. The city walls below were built in the 3rd century BC.

The *phalanx* was a decisive element in the military successes of King Philip of Macedonia. A *phalanx* consisted of heavily armed soldiers who were arranged in rows and armed with a long, heavy spear *(sarissa)* and a relatively short sword. For protection, they wore helmets with cheek and neck guards, a small shield, which during the attack was strung to the thorax, and greaves. This reconstruction shows the infantry charging against the enemy in closed formation.

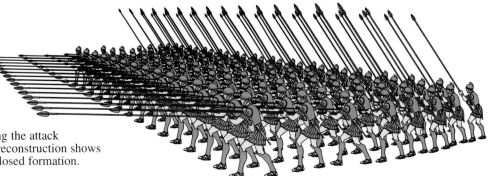

In 1978 archaeologists discovered three royal tombs for members of the Macedonian royal dynasty just outside Vergina (Aigai), the ancient Macedonian capital. During the 1980s the largest tomb (4th century BC) was examined, yielding an unique panoply, made of iron and embellished with the royal emblems – a shining star and lion's head – in gold. The bronze greaves reflect the uneven length of the warrior's legs.

Detail of the 'Sosias' cup (c. 500 BC), which shows the solidarity among soldiers who are treating their wounds. Here Achilles is helping the wounded Patroklos.

Greeks fighting for powers other than their own city against whoever might be the 'enemy', as long as they were paid. Still, for a long time, in the fourth century, the citizen hoplites held their own against the new forces. First Sparta after its victory over Athens, then, by applying a new battle order while still using its own citizens as hoplites, Thebes held a precarious hegemony in Greece.

Meanwhile the new shape of things to come hailed from Macedonia in the north. There, King Philip created a professional army recruited from among the citizens and financed from recently acquired gold mines. It fought as a new-style heavy infantry in battalions called *phalanges*. Armed with pikes of some four meters (12 feet) long which needed handling with both arms and thus drastically reduced the size of the shield that was attached to the left elbow, these troops could, in progressive ranks, literally sweep any opponent off the battlefield. To them was added a more or less professional cavalry recruited from among the

Doctor Iapyx removing an arrow point from the thigh of Aeneas, the Trojan hero and legendary founder of Rome.
The Roman poet Virgil relates that the wound was then treated with a mixture of marjoram, picked by the goddess Venus herself... This fresco from Pompeii realistically portrays this episode.

Stèlè commemorating Caius Largennius, born in Italy, who died in the army camp of Argentorate (Strasbourg) at the age of 37 after 18 years of active service as a legionary.

Macedonian gentry. In 338 BC, Philip defeated the combined armies of Athens and Thebes and in doing so virtually brought the era of the citizen hoplites to a close. Nearly the whole of Greece had to acknowledge his leadership. His son Alexander then led the Macedonian army, strengthened by mercenaries and contingents from Greece, against the Persian Empire (334-323 BC) for the great campaign of revenge, glory and conquest with which a new era began: Hellenism.

In the Hellenistic Age (late fourth till late first century BC), war was a professional business. The armies of the states in Europe, Asia and Egypt that originated in Alexander's conquests consisted of professional soldiers, whether mercenaries from abroad or Greek or Macedonian settlers in the newly conquered territories. They fought in Macedonian-style *phalanges*, in battalions of light-armed troops or in regiments of cavalry. It was an age of diversification of armies, even of experiments (with the use of elephants from India, for example). Battles became more complicated, depending on the cooperation of various 'arms'. Logistics and strategy demanded attention and generals could excel more clearly than in the simple tactics of hoplite battles. Thus, the Hellenistic Age became the time of the great strategists and tacticians. Siege warfare reached its apogee, and the building of fortresses and walls, however much developed, could not keep pace with it. For the first time, science and technique were applied to war in a somewhat systematic way and theoretical treatises on the art of war were being published. The armies of the great monarchies in Egypt, Syria or Macedonia were naturally much bigger than those of the classical city-states (numbering up to 70,000 or 80,000) yet represented a much smaller fraction of the population. For, characteristic of the age, there was a virtual disarmament of the citizens, and certainly of the subjugated Oriental populations, now that war was in the hands of the professionals. Armies had become the instruments of governments and kings, and vast territories could be

Replica of the *valetudinarium*, or hospital of a Roman legion in Vetera (Xanten, Germany), made by R. Schultze. Hospitals built during the 1st and 2nd centuries would invariably be made up of three wings with 60 rooms and a wing with the entrance, kitchen, baths and operation rooms. All wings were situated around a patio.

The golden age of galleys

About 5,000 years ago in Egypt the first known wooden warship appeared; a galley which combined a square-rigged sail, for long distances, and forty oarsmen for a fast attack on the enemy. The fore and aft decks were raised for archers and spearthrowers and some ships had a fender above the water line.

Crete formed an organized navy with Egypt in 2000 BC to combat piracy. Five hundred years later there was a marked difference between merchant vessels, the slow 'round ship', and the *unireme* (Latin *remus*, 'oar'), the narrow, fast one-master with sharp curved stems and one tier of oarsmen. In 1100 BC the Phoenicians became the dominant sea power in the Mediterranean. Their galleys had two tiers of oarsmen *(bireme)* and were long in the bows with a high stern. The fender (Greek, *embolon*) was now on or under the water line. This was the most important type of warship in 1000-500 BC. The Greeks also went over to biremes around 700 BC, when the maximum length (65 feet, 50 oarsmen each side) of their single-decked *pentekonter* was attained. A few generations later the trireme appeared, a fast galley (7-9 knots) measuring 130 by 13 feet with a crew of 200, including 170 oarsmen in three tiers and a small group of heavily armed sailors. Even on this slim maneuverable ship there was little room for victuals, so that it had to go into a port every night.

Tactics were fairly rudimentary: two columns of galleys tried to destroy each other by ramming and boarding each others' vessels. In 500 BC there was also the *diekplous*, the breaking through of the enemy's line, followed by an attack to the flank, and the *periplous*, the widening of the battle line so far that the enemy could be taken on its vulnerable flank. After the Battle of Salamis (480 BC), where these tactics were applied, the trireme became the backbone of the fleets of the various Greek states. At the end of the fourth century, Demetrius I Poliorcetes of Macedonia further equipped the archers with heavy projectiles, catapults and ballistas, making it possible to attack from a greater distance. The ships were also made faster by setting more oarsmen to every oar.

Rome traditionally had a land army, but throughout the Punic Wars from 264 BC onwards, it was forced to develop as a sea power. Roman *corvus* galleys were fitted out with a falling gangplank and grappling hook. Grappling tactics were more important than ramming and led to great success at the Battle of Mylae (Sicily), where 44 Carthaginian ships and 10,000 men were defeated.

After the Second Punic War, Rome was supreme at sea and the conventional fully decked ramming galley made its return, fitted with spritsail *(artemon)*, two archery towers and a grappling iron *(harpax)*, which could also be catapulted. For sailing in convoy and combatting pirates a lighter unireme made its entrance. This more than 97,5 feet long *navis liburna* (Greek, dromon, 'sprinter') would remain in use far into Byzantine times. The last galleys only made their exit at the end of the eighteenth century.

Roman galley from c. 35 BC.

dominated by expert troops in small garrisons. There was no longer any organic link between the military and the populace at large. In the vicissitudes of war, huge areas could easily be carved out or overrun by rivals or foreign peoples. In the end, the Hellenistic states could not resist the pressures from outside. In the east, there were the Iranian peoples, foremost the Parthians, who reconquered the territory up to the Euphrates. The rest fell to the power of Rome.

The Roman expansion

In its early history, Rome was probably quite similar to the Greek city-states. Still, Roman society was more primitive and primitive traits characterized Roman warfare – not only in its semi-magical practices, but also in its tendency to put as many men on the battlefield as possible and to fight its wars, with disregard of most of the rules of the Greek code of war, if possible to the finish. Defeated enemies could be totally exterminated, or enslaved or incorporated into the Roman community itself. Alternatively, states could be forced into an 'alliance' which amounted to a form of submission. These incorporations into the Roman community led to full Roman citizenship immediately or after some generations. It is here that a cardinal difference with the Greek city can be observed. In Greece, a ruling city hardly ever granted citizenship to foreigners; in Rome, it was a simple matter. The explanation may lie in the social structure of Rome, where equality of the citizens counted for less than the vertical links between the mighty and the low. Consequently, it was in the interest of the mighty to cast their nets of patronage still wider.

Under the kings (till c. 500 BC), Rome was a powerful community in the heart of the Italian peninsula. After some setbacks against neighboring peoples in the first age of the Republic, during the second half of the fourth century, a period of practically unbroken expansion began. The *civitas Romana* spread by force through central Italy, then to the north and to the south of the peninsula. Growth of the Roman citizenry meant

Elephants were used in warfare by the Carthaginian general Hannibal during the Punic Wars he fought with the Romans. The objective of this tactic was to deter the infantry, but the animals soon proved to be very difficult to maintain. Plate from Campania, 3rd century BC.

The so-called 'Mars of Todi' gives a picture of the panoply in the time of the early Republic Roman legionaries (4th century BC). Helmet, shield and spear have been lost over the ages, but the structure of the harness, which at the time consisted of leather with metal plates, shows that it is an improved version of the rigid bronze thorax of archaic Greece.

growth of the Roman citizen army. At the beginning of the Republic the normal levy or legio had numbered some 3,000 infantry equipped in the manner of hoplites and fighting in a Roman *phalanx* formation, while the sons of the aristocracy provided a small cavalry. Starting in the fourth century, *legions* were divisions of the army and nominally 4,200 men strong. The legion now attacked in three waves: first the light-armed with long distance weapons, then the first shock troops with javelins, long shields and swords, lastly and only when necessary the old-fashioned shock troops with spears and swords in the style of the hoplites. This diversified and flexible organization would prove itself superior to the armies of Carthage and the Hellenistic monarchies in the third and second centuries BC.

Around 270 BC, the whole of the peninsula south of the river Po was directly or indirectly under Roman rule. About one quarter of its territory and one third of its population had become Roman, the rest as 'allies' in varying degrees of dependence, provided, in time of war, at least as many troops as the Roman state itself. It was this reservoir of manpower combined with a doggedness of character that would not shrink from heavy losses in the field that explains to a large extent Roman successes in subsequent wars with the great powers around the Mediterranean. In the murderous Second Punic War (218-201, against Carthage), Roman manpower (up to 20 legions were then under arms) brought Hannibal, the greatest of the Hellenistic generals, to his knees. In the ensuing century large parts of Spain, Southern Gaul, North Africa, Greece and Asia Minor were conquered and divided into provinces.

This expansion eventually caused a dramatic change

in the composition of the Roman army. Traditionally it had been a citizen levy; in the second century, some 40-50% of the citizens actually did wartime service at one moment or other. But the impoverishment of the smaller landowners, due among other things to long-time absence from their lands in the army and to the new competition of rich proprietors (the profiteers of war and booty), together with the ongoing demand from ever new theaters of war, compelled the Roman state first to lower the property qualifications, then, towards the end of the second century, to abolish them altogether. As a result, generals now could replete their legions from the numerous class of proletarians – those sections of the population that had hitherto not been eligible for military service, because they lacked the means to equip themselves properly. These soldiers became in fact professionals, serving for a moderate salary (out of which they had to pay for their own equipment) and often for many years on end, and awaiting from their commanders a pension in the form of a piece of land – and war booty in the meantime. The higher classes withdrew from the ranks and filled the officers corps, with the result that the Roman army, like the Greek armies, became a body of professionals with only weak links to an unarmed citizenry. Politically, this situation undermined the constitutional fabric of the Republic, since the great warlords now had armies at their disposal that were more loyal to their persons than to the abstract notion of 'the state'. An age of blood and iron ensued, in which first the Italian allies acquired the Roman citizenship, thereby more than doubling Roman numbers (c. 80 BC). More countries were then conquered by rival generals who enlarged the state with Syria (64 BC), Gaul (58-52

Emperor Trajan (98-117) addressing his troops. The supreme command was one of the most important responsibilities of the Roman emperor; its delegation to technocrats, along with the increasing numbers of mercenaries, led to the decay of the Roman army. Bas-relief of the Arch of Constantine in Rome.

This *Gemma Augustea* shows Emperor Augustus, crowned with laurels, next to the goddess Roma. At the bottom the vanquished barbarians, whose lives the magnanimous emperor has spared. Roman soldiers erect a trophy, symbol of victory.

BC) and finally Egypt (30 BC). At the same time, the clashes between the generals hammered the old republic into the new mold of the monarchy. It was Octavian, having changed his name to Augustus, who finally founded the empire (30 BC-14 AD), thus 'Hellenizing' Rome in the respect of making its army essentially an instrument of monarchical power.

The Imperial army
Augustus rounded off the Roman conquests in Spain, the Alps and the Balkans. He established a regular system of provincial administration and reorganized the army. The enormous number of legions from the last phase of the civil wars was reduced to twenty-

eight from a total of around sixty at the height of the civil wars, albeit of a nominal strength of henceforth 6,000 men each. By now, the equipment of the legionary soldiers had become standardized and uniform: they wore metal cuirasses and helmets, oblong shields embossed or inlaid with metal, and fought with two rather heavy javelins and, for close combat, a short sword. The main subdivisions of the legion now were the *cohorts*, consisting of six *centuries* each, recruited from the Roman citizenry. Since the number of the latter had grown enormously in the last century, Augustus' legions now represented only about 3% of the population. The army of the Empire also numbered auxiliary troops, both cavalry and infantry, from the provincial populations that still had not received Roman citizenship. The fighting quality of these troops was high as they were commanded by Roman officers. They received, however, just under a legionary's pay. The tendency towards uniformity that had already set in during the late Republic continued under the Empire. As a result, the cohorts of auxiliary infantry could in the second century hardly be distinguished from those of the legions.

The forces of the Roman Empire, some 3-400,000 troops in all, were concentrated in the outer provinces. In the course of time, a system of frontier defense arose, called the *limes* system, in which the legions mainly along the rivers Rhine and Danube, in the East and in Britannia (the last province was joined to the Empire in the middle of the first century) at certain intervals, with auxiliary troops in between. The Roman defense system in the second and early third centuries was a nearly perfect machine with high standards of provision, housing, medical care, logistical organization and troops and officer rotation. The rank and file had better prospects in the army than in society at large. For the elite of the Empire, military service was a more or less obligatory phase in their careers which traditionally conferred high prestige. Tactically, the strength of the Roman army lay in the heavy infantry of its legions and cohorts, although we do not know very much about its actual fighting practices in open battle. For instance, did the legions still operate as fighting units or was that role taken over by the cohorts? But in one way or another, the imperial Roman army still continued the line formation that was first brought to perfection by the early Greek *phalanges*.

Part of the ruins of the army camp in Nijmegen (the Netherlands), where troops of the 10th Roman legion were quartered. The stone construction was built in 90 AD.

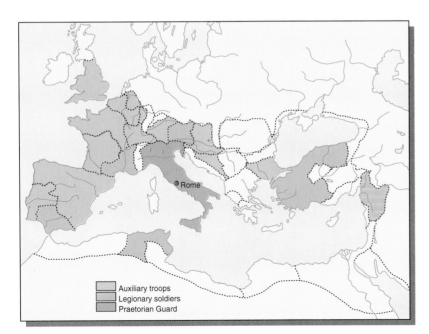

Auxiliary troops
Legionary soldiers
Praetorian Guard

Main areas of recruitment of the Roman army during the rule of Emperor Trajan (98-117). Trajan's army consisted of c. 30 legions, complemented by auxiliary forces and cavalry, totalling around 400,000 troops. Legionaries always had Roman civil rights and mainly originated from the areas which had been ruled by Rome for a considerable period of time. The auxiliary forces were mainly recruited in fringe areas, still by and large un-Romanized, particularly in the border provinces. During the rule of Trajan hardly any legionaries were recruited in Italy itself; only the imperial guard, the Praetorian Guard, was recruited in Italy.

With difficulty soldiers are scaling the city walls by instruction of their superiors who are leading the siege from a distance. Meanwhile an enormous battering ram with a huge iron ball hanging from a chain is being rolled forward to breach the wall. Detail of 'The conquest of Jerusalem by Titus', a painting which illustrates the siege of Ghent at the end of the 15th century.

The art of war in medieval Europe

The Middle Ages are regarded as an era of insecurity and aggression, associated with fortified castles and noble knights. War by the nobility was considered not only a commonplace activity but also a vital, ennobling one, during the course of which there was a chance to display all kinds of virtues and accomplishments. However, lower strata of the population were also called on to campaign when necessary.

Philippe Contamine

In Hastings, on October 14, 1066, the Norman duke William the Conqueror defeated Harold, the successor to the childless English king Edward the Confessor. Crossing the English Channel with horses, provisions, etc. was no easy task. The so-called 'Bayeux Tapestry', which depicts the crossing in beautiful colors, was embroidered shortly after the event.

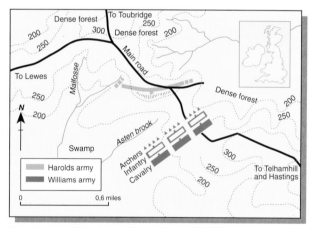

The Battle of Hastings. The nucleus of William's army was its harnessed cavalry. Harold's army mainly consisted of footmen armed with axes, swords and spears, unable to ward off a cavalry attack in open terrain. Therefore, Harold had taken a strong position on top of a steep hillcrest, his flanks covered by woodlands, brooklets and swamps. The Normans did not gain the day and kill Harold until after they had feigned a retreat. They lured the English out into the open, where they were butchered by the cavalry.

The fortified castle (together with the town or city enclosed in stone walls) and the knight (who offers a singularly expressive variety in the form of crusader, Templar, Hospitaller, Teutonic, etc.) figure amongst the small number of images which we commonly associate with our picture of the Middle Ages in Europe – here understood to indicate the extremely long period of time between the fall of the Roman Empire and the Renaissance. In other words, the Middle Ages is regarded as an era of insecurity and aggression. Hence the recourse to a fortified dwelling by individuals, families and communities when this was technically, economically and politically feasible. Hence the privileged position held by warriors at the heart of society so that power was normally their due, or conversely, so that men of power faced the practical obligation of also being warriors, or perhaps of being warriors first and foremost, at least potentially. In the same vein, war was considered not only a commonplace activity but also a vital, ennobling one, during the course of which there was a chance to display all kinds of virtues and accomplishments. Christianity, which then dominated and controlled ways of thinking and institutions, the spheres of public and private life, vigorously condemned certain forms of war and certain types of warrior, but came to acknowledge the probity of other forms, even according them an eminent spiritual value, and setting genuine combatants on its altars.

The art of war

The art of war in feudal times was characterized in the first place by the fact that, at least in conflicts between Christians – by far the most frequent kind – the objective was to pillage, burn, destroy and kill, but in no way to enslave the vanquished. Either the conquered enemy was put to death in the heat of combat (this was even a systematic policy in order to spread terror), a fairly common practice despite provoking indignant reactions from churchmen, or they were taken prisoner, and not just robbed but also only released on payment of ransom. So going to war meant risking death and also ruin. In most cases a prisoner of war

Dover castle, situated on the cliffs high above
the city, dominates the city of Dover and its port. From
1066 Dover was the most important of the *Cinque
Ports*, the five Channel ports which were responsible for
provisioning and maintaining the English fleet.
In return, they were granted certain rights, among them
exemption from taxes.

belonged to an individual who was considered his
master (a war leader or combatant with a certain
social standing, wielding a particular authority), not to
a collective body which we would call a state. It was
quite regular, at the beginning of a campaign or before
battle was engaged, for combatants to undertake to
pool their spoils of war (prisoners and booty) which
would subsequently be shared according to individual
rank and responsibilities. So every martial enterprise
had public, collective and individual aspects.

We can speculate on the reasons for the disappearance, from the High Middle Ages onwards, of the secular link between war and slavery. The appearance of
another mode of production perhaps (but this is not
sufficient to explain the absence of domestic slaves
acquired through war), or possibly an extension of the
idea which made it unthinkable for a Christian warrior
to reduce one of his brothers to servitude, as everyone
had been made free by Christ (we should note, however, that slavery did reappear at this time, to the det-
riment of races from other regions, particularly Afri-
cans, infidels and pagans).
Another characteristic of war in the feudal era was

The struggle
between
David and Goliath,
illustrated
according to
the views
of the
12th century
Spaniards,
at the time when
the Castilians
were waging
war on the
Muslims.

47

Long and heavy coat of mail, made of iron links. After 1200 these coats became shorter. Knights would wear such long protective clothing in battle or during fighting exercises.

that it was conducted by an extremely large number of powers, with widely differing resources, from the Holy Roman Emperor or the King (of France, England, Sicily, Jerusalem, Castile, Léon, etc.) to simple knights with their meager forces and poor funds. In an extremely wide area of Europe every noble deemed he had his own right to conduct war. This right was the expression of his liberty. To a certain extent, major wars conducted by major powers resembled coalitions at the heart of which each participant, small, middling or great, retained his margin of maneuver and initiative. A large war involved the synergy of disparate, heterogenous forces, more or less autonomous, united in a temporary and necessarily precarious fashion, under the authority of a war leader whose troops were

Until c. 1200 helmets were cast in one piece. The part protecting the face was pierced with small holes, and could not be opened. The blazon was painted on the knight's shield; the helmet would also frequently carry his armorial bearings so that they could be recognized in battle. This is an allegorical representation of the victory of modesty over pride.

Lance and shield		
Helmet		
Legguards		
Sword and sheath		
Mail shirt		
Horse		

The cost of a fully armed, mounted knight valued in cows (c. 800).

constantly in danger of disbanding, mutinying and dispersing.

This context explains why the majority of conflicts were of brief duration and mediocre intensity, affecting a relatively restricted area. For the same reason these conflicts brought together limited forces. The stakes appear to us second-rate, incoherent, insignificant, almost derisory; we often have the impression that the people of the era made war for war's sake, as an exercise which was simply part of their way of life, not with any clearly defined strategic aim. War was conducted for pleasure, like hunting. Truth be told, this impression is somewhat misleading. If we examine in detail the martial activities of a feudal figure, we will soon perceive that in their own way these activities were part of a genuine policy, that they were coherent and had their tactical, even strategic, logic.

The administrative and institutional side of feudal war was barely developed, or in any case unobtrusive. The documentation has to be examined attentively in order to spot its existence. We are in the presence of warriors rather than soldiers. If the concept of an army entails notions of bureaucracy and paperwork, we can frankly say that the collections of combatants typical of the period from the tenth to the twelfth century do not have the right to this appellation. The difference is evident if, for example, we compare the armies of the early and late Roman Empire, and also the Byzantine army in the period of Justinian, with the army in the period of the Macedonian emperors. Naturally there were problems of discipline, provisions, logistics, support and remuneration of the combatants, but on a

The *Chanson de Roland*, a French epic which dates back to the late 11th century, relates the withdrawal of Charlemagne from Spain after his defeat at the hands of the Saracens at Roncevalles in 788. When Roland, who was with the rearguard, was attacked from behind in the Pyrenees, he blew his horn 'Elephant' in dire need as a final call for assistance. Unfortunately, Charlemagne did not come to his rescue on time. This scene is the theme of this Flemish miniature, made c. 1458.

reduced scale, for which empirical solutions, largely improvised, were found as occasion demanded.

Wars were as numerous as they were feeble in import. However, several were expressions of unquestionable ambition and savoir faire. The conquest of England by William the Conqueror, Duke of Normandy, the seizure of this quite extensive, rich and populated territory, is a clear example. It was an enterprise which demanded the co-operation of thousands of more or less voluntary combatants, recruited over a quite considerable area, with horsemen (the knights) alongside archers; it demanded the assembly of a fleet of hundreds of ships, a fleet capable of transporting men and arms and also horses (a real technical achievement, also repeated during the crusades). William's victory at Hastings on October 14, 1066, as crushing as it was, did not put an end to all resistance, however. He was obliged to seize towns, bring the insurgents to heel, employ systematic devastation throughout the north of the country, build large numbers of castles to serve as a communication network (the Tower of London being his masterpiece) and organize the remuneration and define the military obligations of hundreds, or rather thousands, of knights, some directly main-

The remains of the medieval castle of La Bâtiaz in Martigny, situated opposite the 'knee of the river Rhône', testify to the great strategic importance this castle used to have, located at a junction of roads from the Simplon pass to the Great St. Bernard pass.

tained by nobles or the king, others granted fiefs from which they were supposed to draw their living.

The battle

The fact remains, however, that the majority of conflicts took the form of simple guerilla activities (destruction, pillage, ambush), or defending or attacking fortresses, which were often situated on the frontiers of opposing spheres of domination. According to the soie piece of written documentation, these fortified castles and towns were fairly scattered: there were less than a hundred, for example, in the vast duchy of Normandy in the twelfth century. However, as we follow the

thread of time their numbers increase, and recent archaeological research has made it possible to identify an impressive number of minor fortifications, in wood or stone. The best known of these rudimentary fortifications were the feudal *mottes*. However, scholars agree that their function was as much symbolic as military. So at the strategic level, the important fortifications were the ones mentioned in the texts. These fortifications kept abreast of developments in warfare by tirelessly perfecting their systems of defense, while in a parallel process castles were built *ex nihilo*, at great expense, obviously to conform with the latest in military techniques (for example, the Welsh fortresses of Edward I of England). From the tenth to the thirteenth century, siege operations became increasingly complex and sophisticated. The use of mines, trenches, siege towers and catapult artillery entailed the deployment of technical personnel, veritable military engineers. The besieged forces also employed all these processes, while their task was to defend an increasingly coherent and interdependent ensemble for as long as their water, provisions and munitions lasted. In order to win in a

These people are begging God to intervene, to repel the pursuit
and siege, while a handful of archers and lancers are defending the gate.
Detail of a miniature from the Utrecht *Psalter*, late 12th century.

The fortress of Carcassonne (Languedoc) dates back to 1150, and was built on the remains of a Moorish castle. During the following centuries, a double defensive wall was contiguously erected around the town, c. 1 mile long, with 52 bastions and 2 gates. From 1844 onwards the fortress and walls were restored to their old glory by the architect Viollet-le-Duc.

Moorish strongholds

After the death of the Visigoth king Witiza in 709 a civil war started on the Iberian peninsula between the camps of the pretenders to the throne, Favila and Roderick. Followers of Favila enlisted the aid of the governor Mûsâ ibn Nusayr in 711, who sent his general Tariq ibn Ziyad over the straits of Gibraltar with an army of Berbers who within only a few years managed to drive the Visigoths to the north. The Moors then held sway over present-day Spain and Portugal until the *Reconquista* was completed by the exiled Christians in 1492.

The Arabic conquistadors were the first to build the extensive fortifications which played such an important role in town construction in central and southern Spain. These *alcazabas* (fortified palaces) formed part of the city walls (in Córdoba, Seville and Saragossa) or a citadel (the Alhambra in Grenada). They were built on strategic hills in Malaga, Alméria, Alicante, Lérida, Carmora and Ronda. Where there were no ramparts (Seville, Córdoba) a fortified home (*ksar*, Spanish: *alcazar*) was built for the local ruler.

The natural state of the terrain determined the form of the Moorish strongholds, which were characterized by enormous walls flanked by towers. The poor quality of the building material (a mixture of cement and gravel) necessitated four or more towers that were cornered, in contrast to the semi-circular European towers. The use of air-dried brick also did very little to improve the durability of the buildings. Immediately after the Recon-

quista, some castles were still in use by the Castilians, but very soon the majority was demolished or rebuilt as fortified monasteries (as in Calutrava and Loarre). Earthquakes (1755) and the growth of the cities also contributed to the demolition of Moorish architecture.

Of the *Castillo Moro* in Gibraltar (from the eighth century) only ruins remain. In Guadix (in Andalusia) parts of the city wall (including the Moorish city gates) and the *alcazaba* can be seen. Toledo still has fortifications dating from this period. Seville is still in proud possession of the *Toro del Oro* (1228), the 'Golden' Moorish watchtower, and the brick Giralda tower (c. 1100), a 100 m (325 ft) high former minaret and watchtower, now part of the cathedral. The only places where the visitor can truly sense Moorish times are the *Mezquita* (950-987) in Córdoba (with 340 columns and 36 domes) and the Alhambra in Grenada with its *alcazaba* (1240), the *Palacio Araba* (1350) and the *Patio Leones* (1377).

In Portugal too, most Moorish citadels (Lisbon, Santarém) and mosques were demolished or used as foundations for other buildings after the Reconquista. In Sintra stand the ruins of the Pena palace (with Moorish domes) and a Moorish castle from the eighth century. By contrast the citadel near the fishing village of Sesimbra has been completely restored. In Silves the large cistern of the Moorish fort is back in use and in Mertola one can recognize the Moorish influence in the splendid arches and winding streets. All these remains only offer a glimpse of the former beauty of Moorish culture in Europe.

The walls around the Moorish citadel of Niebla, a city between Sevilla and Huelva, strategically situated on a hill over the main road to Portugal.

situation where it was not always possible to create an effective blockade, and aware of the dangers of any frontal attack, the besieging forces preferred surprise or negotiation; the besieged garrison would undertake to surrender the stronghold, provided they were allowed to leave unharmed, with arms, baggage and mount. Often a date for surrender had been fixed: if no relief army had arrived by this time, the garrison would open its gates, considering that this failure to come to their aid released them from both their moral and legal obligations.

A solemn and perilous event, often regarded as a kind of judgment from God, the battle (the pitched battle,

the appointed or public battle) survived in a much more episodic fashion. In practical terms, it was necessary for both parties to be in agreement to meet in a bloody clash, the outcome of which no one could predict. Often each army was split into three divisions, for simultaneous or successive engagement. Diversions and wheeling movements, from the left or right wing, were employed. Each corps maneuvered in a specific number of units, only two or three ranks in depth, grouped around banners, later standards. Combatants were required to keep together as much as possible (and therefore adopt a passive attitude, consisting of stubborn resistance) while at the same time

Shipping troops, horses and ordnance was a task which demanded a good logistical organization and at times quite a lot of improvisation. Sea travel was usually safe, and sometimes much faster than travel through enemy areas, but it was above all very expensive. This miniature (c. 1480) shows the French fleet leaving for Castile.

The success of the parties in the Hundred Years' War between England and France varied with their fortune. This is the Battle of Poitiers (1356), which saw the numerically inferior English, led by the 'Black Prince', vanquish the superior numbers of the French, under the command of the Dauphin. A particularly successful tactic which the English used consisted in simultaneously shooting a deluge of arrows with a wide arc into the front ranks.

attacking the enemy line in order to disrupt its grouping. Once the grouping of a line had been disrupted, the battle corps would disintegrate in panic and flee. These were the only occasions when great massacres and prisoner round-ups would occur.

The feudal Middle Ages were not familiar with the concept of conscription *stricto sensu*. War was not just the business of young men. It was generally agreed that clerics and members of religious orders could not serve under arms, apart from exceptional circumstances. However, to an eminently variable degree, the population as a whole, both in town and country, was not exempt from all military service. The peasants on a castle domain, the villeins on a manorial fief, could be called on to campaign, in a subordinate or support capacity, at least for several days. They were not prohibited from carrying arms. The situation was similar in urban communities. Every citizen was a potential warrior, whose deployment by parish, profession or quarter was determined in time of peace. Each urban unit was entrusted with the defense of a specific part of the town wall.

Knights

The heart of the medieval host, however, was formed by representatives of the noble classes, in the broadest sense of the term, i.e. knights, to simplify the situation a little. A feudal host ordinarily consisted of several hundred heavily armed knights, each of whom was

The fortress of 'Rocca Fregoso' (10th-15th century) at Sant' Agata Feltria (near Montefeltro), along with numerous other fortresses in the same area, testifies to the countless hostilities and wars fought out in this area throughout the Middle Ages. The longest and most bitter struggle was between the Montefeltro family from Urbino and the Malatesta family from Rimini.

During the course of the 13th century, military leaders began to assume offices of civil authority in many cities in northern and central Italy. This development resulted in a system of – often hereditary – autocracy during the 14th and 15th centuries. Memorial from 1329 for Giangrande della Scala, ruler of Verona.

'The battle of San Romano', painted c. 1456 by Paolo Uccello, depicts the height of the struggle between Florence and Siena. Here the Sienese commander is wounded. Uccello depicted all types of weaponry: crossbows, lances, harnesses, caparisons and feathered helmets.

The Duke of Brabant's troops arriving at Ravenstein at sunset. Miniature from Jean Froissarts' *Chroniques*, made in Bruges c. 1480.

accompanied at the very least by a squire, a sergeant at arms and three horses. Inevitably, they fought alongside foot soldiers, including archers and crossbowmen, and also the 'rabble' who could turn their hand to any task and were renowned less for their effectiveness than for their cupidity, lack of discipline and cruelty. They were volunteers, after all, even if they had been supplied by medieval communities.

The accent should therefore be placed on the knights. Some were recruited, equipped and maintained by nobles of high rank, but the majority of knights supported themselves with their own resources, derived from the revenues from their fiefs. They did not expect any remuneration from their employers, their leaders, until they had completed their service, 'to defray costs'. Their lance, their sword, their hauberk and their charger formed their capital – a precarious capital at the mercy of a raid or an epidemic. These knights, whose coat of arms was reproduced on their pennon, shield, tunic, and horse's caparison (to identify them and supposedly to incite them to courage), underwent fairly intensive military training as a rule,

which was in fact more individual than collective. Jousts, tournaments and other mock battle encounters were an apprenticeship in war, as was hunting.

Knights were experienced warriors, specialist fighters who were meant to be inspired by both the audacity of Knight Roland and the prudence of the wise Oliver. Their social and professional standing was officially sanctified by the rite of admission – undoubtedly very ancient – which took the form of dubbing, the 'new knighthood'. Traditional military virtues were set before them and recommended (including 'knightly discipline', the forerunner of military discipline). And within the framework of the crusade and doctrines concerning God's Peace, the Church progressively prescribed an elevated (and naturally utopian) ideal of fighting for good and for justice against the forces of evil; protecting orphans, the poor, women, merchants, monks, pilgrims ... We have now arrived at the origin of *ius in bello*, a concept beyond the war of people, goods, time and place. In its purest form the knightly ideal was very close to the ideal associated with kings. The knight's sword, in Christian images of the soldier, was the sword of justice. Significantly, certain forms of dubbing almost acquired the aspect of coronations or consecrations, while coronations and consecrations included a kind of dubbing in their ritual.

Changes and innovations

Although there was never any kind of decisive break, properly speaking, the last two or three centuries of the Middle Ages introduced a certain number of changes and innovations. War, with its elements of ransom and booty, certainly remained a private adventure for those who engaged in it. However, states (we shall use this term even if it is not entirely appropriate) made perceptible attempts to control the spoils of war mechanism, in order to appropriate the profits, and, more importantly, to have a more disciplined and effective military instrument at their disposal.

Between 1300 and 1500 the number of powers capable of conducting a war on their own account decreased drastically, thanks to the development of political entities who, irrespective of their scale or character, claimed to reserve for themselves the monopoly of war – of legitimate violence, to use the celebrated phrase – and therefore the monopoly of their subjects' defense. In France at the end of the fifteenth century, the nobles' right of 'private' war had virtually disappeared; when the king clashed with the Duke of Brittany it was a war of state against state. Not all the West benefitted from this simplification of the conflict map: in Germany, for example, the 'feudal' tradition remained deplorably hardy. With fewer and fewer actors on the stage of war, conflicts became longer, bringing together better trained forces (despite the demographic crisis) for strategic missions that were better defined, or at least more comprehensible.

The introduction of the longbow, the improvements made to the crossbow, the invention of the flail, then the arquebus, the mass use of pikes, halberds and other shafted weapons by foot soldiers who were not very mobile but disciplined, could only be a threat, immediate or long-term, to the primacy of mounted soldiers, the cavalry, and therefore of the knight. However, even around 1500, the armies of the West consisted of 'armed men' who, together with their mounts, were better protected than ever. It was a class of warrior in which the aristocratic mentality dominated. The light cavalry was also being employed. Fire or powder artillery, which spread through the West during the fourteenth century (from the 1330s onwards), began to play a notable role in siege warfare in the final quarter of the fourteenth century, and in pitched battles from the first decades of the fifteenth century.

In a century and a half, the progress made in terms of quality and quantity by artisans of exceptional competence was remarkable and almost incessant. The cannons carried on board Atlantic ships and Mediterranean galleys from the final quarter of the fourteenth century were to revolutionize the course of naval battles, before any concept of the warship had been clearly defined.

There were clear social changes as well, although these took fairly varied forms, according to the region.

Edward III, King of England, with his son, the Black Prince, entered the fallen city of Caen in July 1346. Their troops sacked the city for three days.

Looting, but also rape, murder and arson were often the lot of the ordinary citizens of a fallen city; such was the right of the conqueror.

In a considerable area of the West, the population as a whole became much more removed from the scene of combats. In other words, a new stage developed in the professionalization of war, with foot soldiers recruited amongst people of widely different backgrounds (young men out for fun, marginal figures, adventurers), and horse soldiers who were also of highly contrasting social origin, although with a strong noble tone. Around 1500 the organic link between the nobility and war still survived: nobles served, even on a voluntary basis, in the artillery and infantry (and not

The Swiss town of Murten has retained a large part of its medieval fortifications. After an unsuccessful siege of the city in 1476, Duke Charles the Bold consented to outright war with the Swiss confederates.

just at officer level). However, the role of the feudal regime in providing fighting men had been completely undermined.

Almost everywhere in the fifteenth century there were permanent military elements, or elements tending to permanence: the paid fighters or mercenaries, the soldiers (a word related to ancient and modern romance language words for money and pay), who caused moralists of the commonwealth such concern to no avail. The states considered them to be necessary and profitable; they devoted a major portion of their resources to maintaining such troops (together with fortifications and alliances with a military purpose). Tax paying citizens either resigned themselves to this situation or even saw advantages in it. In several European countries, therefore, a military society was born, with its administration and financing, its problems of accommodation, discipline and career.

There was increasing discussion of the craft of war, the science of arms. The first original treatises on war machines, military architecture, tactics, institutions and discipline appeared. Old oral guidelines, supplemented by rare manuscripts from the ancient Romans, were now decidedly insufficient. Charles the Bold's series of military orders set forth a quantity of unedited formulas on hierarchy, the transmission of commands, major and minor maneuvers. There was a renaissance of the art of war; Machiavelli was only one of its representatives.

We should note, however, that this renaissance had its limitations: when later military historians (from Louvois to Frederick II) examined the function and behavior of the armies of Matthias Corvin, Charles VIII, Maximilian Habsburg or even Francisco Sforza, they tended to consider them still as 'feudal' armies. While emerging from the Middle Ages, Europe had a comparatively effective military instrument at its disposal – both on land and sea. It was this instrument which was the particular downfall of the Moorish kingdom of Grenada, which allowed the establishment of Portuguese trading colonies, and later the conquest of the New World. Nevertheless, around 1500, many western observers considered the primary military power more than ever to be the Ottoman Empire, whose incomparable janissaries combined religious conviction and a complete lack of family ties and roots with a sober lifestyle and drill.

Diebold Schilling's *Great Chronicle of Burgundy* contains c. 200 pen drawings, painted in watercolors, depicting episodes from the struggle of the Confederates against Charles the Bold. This is the battle of Murten on June 12, 1476, when Charles suffered a major defeat.

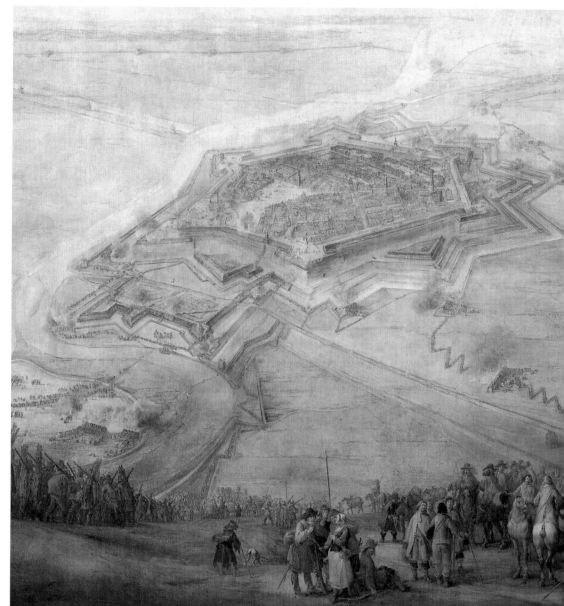

Bastion fortifications

'Modern style' fortifications, invented in sixteenth century Italy and exported to the rest of Europe and the colonies, were so widespread and long-lasting as to leave an indelible and uniform impression particularly on the urban landscapes of Europe: from Scandinavia to the islands of the Mediterranean, from the Iberian peninsula to the eastern borders of the continent. Polygonal towns, boundary walls, isolated bastions and bulwarks have remained more or less intact to the present day.

Maria Nadia Covini

The impressive 15th century stronghold of Coca (province of Segovia) dates from an era when strongholds had an exclusively defensive role. This brick fortress was built by Muslim engineers by order of Alfonso de Fonseca, archbishop of Seville. Archers could shoot arrows from the battlements, and cannons could be fired from the loopholes.

The need to defend

The cannon was invented at the beginning of the fourteenth century and in the following century it became such a powerful offensive weapon that it made any kind of traditional fortification ineffective and obsolete. The 'modern type' of fortification was first tried out in Italy between the fifteenth and sixteenth centuries and the first bastion fortifications, built according to a model which was to become very widespread, with regular geometric shapes and low polygonal bastions, date back to around 1530. Bastions were solid platforms which projected outwards from the wall. The artillery, which was located on the flanks of the bastions, could strike the area in front of adjacent walls with cross shots. The artillery on the platform and on the front of the bastions aimed their fire straight at their attackers. The multiplicity of firing points, and the angular shape of the bastion, allowed the entire area surrounding the fortress to be covered without leaving any blind corners. The perimeter, fortified with bastions, was surrounded by a wide moat, which kept the attackers at a distance and connected the fortress to other strongholds, and along which ran a counterscarp with a covered roadway. The area around the fortification was flattened and cleared to ensure the attackers had no place to hide and to keep the field of fire clear. The bastions were generally made of strong materials, stone and more often bricks, which covered solid earthworks of sand or soil.

History has it that the testing of new techniques was speeded up as a result of the fear in Italy of the powerful French army led by Charles VIII in 1494: an army of 18,000 men accompanied by siege artillery which was impressive not only because of its size – at least

This splendid representation (c. 1514) of the destructive force of a cannonball explosion was depicted by Leonardo da Vinci, famed for, among other things, his numerous military designs.

When Henry VIII landed in Calais in 1520 to negotiate with his French opponent François I, salutations were fired by the guns of the local fortress. Detail of the painting 'The Field of the Cloth of Gold'.

forty large caliber bombards – but mainly because of its mobility, firing speed and range. Although the role played by artillery in the 1494 campaign was fairly limited, it is true that the financial and organizational muscle of the large monarchies determined the spread of these new weapons and gave a strong impetus to research into new methods of defense.

The first bastioned constructions built in the form which was to become a prototype for the rest of Europe were designed by Italian architects, the most prominent of whom were Michele Sammicheli and Antonio da Sangallo il Giovane, who built them in the northern and central states of Italy. Since the fifteenth century, the political situation in these areas had been favorable to experimentation: many hostile and competing states existed, with many frontiers to defend, and the new princes needed citadels to ensure the loyalty of cities which had become accustomed to autonomy and grandeur. In 1534, the new Duke of Florence, Alessandro de'Medici, began to construct the *Fortezza da Basso*, with the stated intention of bridling the city and protecting the medicean state under the tutelage of Emperor Charles V. The Florentine fortress was not one of the most technically innovative constructions but it did mark the beginning of an era because it was an instrument of political and social control.

The Italian environment was also open to experimentation for cultural reasons. Military architects were

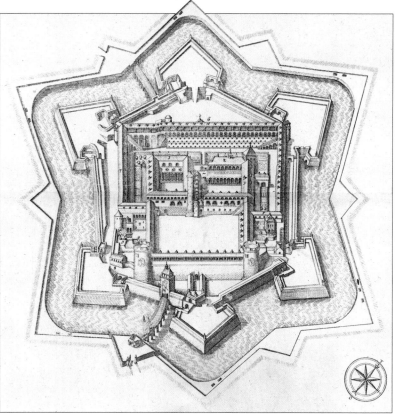

The development of artillery, and the use of more powerful cannons, led to the addition of new fortifications to old castles in the form of the triangular bastion. These bastions can be clearly distinguished on this plan of the Sforza castle in Milan.

Rocroi was among the first cities to be
surrounded by a rampart during the reign of François I,
after the example of Lucca in Italy.

highly regarded and their reputation was no lesser
than that of the major artists of the time. Even Leonardo da Vinci and Michelangelo Buonarroti, among
others, offered cities and princes the benefits of their
expertise as fortress builders.

The history of fortification in the modern era is pri-
marily a history of the genius of military engineers
and architects who, from the fifteenth century onwards, created unique prototypes, invented ingenious
devices and, in their research, took many a potentially
successful route before arriving at the winning solution: the polygonal bastion. This type of fortification
was a considerable innovation, so much so that it radically transformed the concept of permanent defense.
In the fifteenth century, fortifications were static structures which used the size or awkward angles of their
walls in a passive way to counter any projectile
attacks. The new bastioned shapes turned fortifications into real war machines, built not only to defend
but also to counterattack and assail the enemy. Despite
this, not all the ancient fortifications became obsolete.
Some fortresses of the late Middle Ages which were
impressive and strong were modified by various addi-
tions and remained unconquerable for many years. On
the other hand, many of the structures built in the sixteenth century could hardly have been described as
models of refined design or masterpieces of geometry.
They were built hurriedly, using non-durable materials, to deal with concrete threats. They often turned

Rampart
and detached
spearhead-
shaped bastion
of the fortress
of Berwick-
on-Tweed on the
border between
England and
Scotland,
built after an
Italian example
in 1558-1568.

The
Spandau
citadel near
Berlin,
with its
16th century
bastion,
was built after
an Italian
model as
well.

In the 16th century the Italian concepts of fortification reached the Netherlands. During the years of war with Spain, the Dutch built a system of earthen ramparts and bastions, surrounded by moats. In these moats ravelins were built, small pentagonal islets, on which cannons could be placed behind parapets. The entire system was surrounded by a second line of defense. Here the fortified city of Heusden on the river *Bergse Maas* on the southern border of the province of Holland.

out to be short-lived and ineffective. Sometimes, however, where they were supported by natural formations or integrated fortification systems, and despite the coarseness of the design and ineffective pieces of apparatus, they provided distinguished service.

From the second half of the sixteenth century, all the major European states promoted large-scale fortress building programs to defend their frontiers and to create refuges for their armies. The main reason for this flurry of fortress building was the danger of attack by the Turks. Although fortifications were secondary to the formation of fleets, they were built throughout the Mediterranean area in the form of fortified outposts, strongholds or garrisons, particularly along the Adriatic and Ionian coasts, the southern coast of Spain and the northern coast of Africa. The island of Malta, which was attacked by the Turkish fleet in 1564 with a fierce strike which sent a shiver through Mediterranean Europe, was fortified with the assistance of the entire Christian world between 1566 and 1571. Along the southern coast of Italy, which was subjected to

Turkish attacks and barbarian raids, the Spanish Viceroys built a string of coastal towers and maritime strongholds. In its overseas dominions, Venice erected permanent defenses in Dalmatia, Corfu and Crete, and fortified the eastern borders of Friuli.

The creation of fortified frontier settlements was promoted by the French king Francis I who, from 1536, employed some of the most respected Italian engineers to fortify the northern borders of his kingdom. In very little time fifteen strongholds had been built along the border with the Netherlands, defended by over one thousand pieces of artillery. Vitry-le-François, Villefranche sur Meuse and Rocroi, in the Ardennes, were prototype city fortresses which set the standards for future structures of this kind. Similar ones were erected by the Habsburgs on the other side of the border: at Marienburg (1546) and Philippeville (1553).

The greatest number of bastioned structures and fortifications were built, over a period of fifty years, in the Netherlands, where – during the struggle of the Protestant provinces against the Spaniards – approximately 26 miles of modern defenses, four citadels and

In 1591, modern artillery painlessly reduced to rubble the medieval walls of the city of Deventer. After the end of the Eighty Years' War in 1648, the city was surrounded by impressive, modern defenses, which included earthen bastions.

numerous bastioned walls were built on both sides to defend cities and settlements. Military engineers created impressive boundary walls with bastions and monumental doors for the Habsburg and Nassau families and for certain cities such as Breda and Antwerp. Italian engineers also worked in Eastern Europe, in the African colonies and America. At the end of the sixteenth century, the *trace italienne* was the dominant theme in fortifications and had become a truly 'international style'.

In sixteenth century Europe, considerable interest, and

in some cases real enthusiasm, was aroused by the modern technologies of fortification. A demanding fortification plan, or a fortress built according to the latest specifications of military engineers, was the most effective way in which a state could assert its political leadership. Widespread interest in fortification in sixteenth and seventeenth century Europe is witnessed by the flourishing of treatises on military architecture and collections of fortress plans. A wealth of material was published. Treatises and collections of drawings, some original, some reproduced and reviewed, were published throughout Europe, circulating images, ideas and techniques on a grand scale.

The protagonists of this exceptional spread of ideas, which was in itself a small cultural revolution, were the military architects, who were intent on providing their profession with more precise statutes than the general *magistri* of the late Middle Ages. During the sixteenth century, military architects were, by necessity, somewhat eclectic figures. The best among them were not only artists but also humanists and technical experts with an ever increasing knowledge of the subject. Mathematics and geometry, the laws of ballistics and knowledge of previous traditions all formed part of their complex cultural knowledge, which they developed as a result of the experience gained directing labor at the work site. The skills developed in the construction of fortresses and in the preparation of siege structures distinguished professional architects from the endless number of dilettantes and amateurs who also contributed – albeit in a repetitive and scarcely original way – to the impressive proliferation of works and treatises.

The cannon

At the beginning of the fourteenth century, the introduction of gunpowder in Europe caused a revolution in the technology of projectile weapons, although older weapons (the bow, the spear and the ballista) would remain in use for a long time. The cannon was probably invented in 1313 by the Augustinian monk Berthold Schwarz from Freiburg. When it was first used is debatable. Florentine documents from 1326 are the first to mention the purchase of cannons for the defense of Florence and from then on this weapon was known throughout Western Europe.

Cannons were cast in bronze or made of wrought iron (from the fourteenth century) and cast iron (from 1520). The technique of casting was already known in the making of clocks. Wrought iron was cheaper than bronze, but of a lower quality. In the beginning every cannon was unique, had its own name and in Italy even the cannonballs were engraved.

In the fifteenth century people tried to build still bigger supercannons, which were only effective in sieges and for the defense of cities. The Turks used these weapons for taking Constantinople in 1453. In Western Europe it is still possible to see the 5 ton, 50 caliber *Mons Meg* in Edinburgh and the 700 pounder, 13 ton *Dulle Griet* in Ghent.

The forming of national states and the battles which accompanied this, however, required a smaller, more mobile artillery. Charles VIII of France (1483-1498) placed his light cannons on an undercarriage which could be pulled by horses. This model was quickly reloadable and on level ground could keep up with the infantry reasonably well, which appears from the invasion of Italy (1494). The battles at Ravenna (1512) and Marignano (1515) were the first where field artillery played a decisive role. The sixteenth century saw the appearance of cast iron cannons in England, Holland and Sweden, the standardization of ammunition and caliber and the development of ballistics. After technological improvements in the century that followed, cast iron was used more often. Amsterdam became Europe's largest munitions market and European production potential greatly increased. The eighteenth century brought further uniformity of design, the addition of the hand-drawn cart for transporting munitions, tools, spare parts and gun crew, and the division according to mobility of cavalry, field and garrison artillery.

Cannons began to play a more and more crucial role in battle; a reason why Napoleon promoted his cannoneers to an elite corps. Technical improvements in the nineteenth century were Alfred Krupp's rotating one-piece steel cannon (1851), the breechloader (1860) and a hydraulic counterblow mechanism. The greater range made firing from the back lines possible. During World War I the German cannon 'Big Bertha' was able to bombard Paris from a distance of 122 km (73 mile). Since the introduction of the tank, the tactical bomber and more recently guided missiles, the role of artillery has been reduced. Yet even late in the twentieth century some war-minded statesmen have still attempted to introduce even mightier artillery.

French gunners from the 2nd half of the 17th century. Litho by Gustave David (1824-1891).

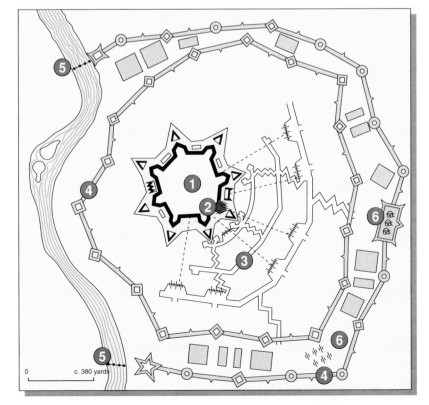

Palmanova

One of the most well known examples is the city-fortress of Palmanova, erected by the Republic of Venice from 1593. As with many fortifications of the time, Palmanova was not the masterpiece of only one mind, but the result of many different contributions borne out of very different technical, cultural and ideological premises. The construction of Palmanova saw the contribution of Buonaiuto Lorini, a military architect and theorist who had worked in various European countries and who was well informed about the latest

The siege of a 17th or 18th century stronghold was a lengthy and complicated task. The besieger's first move was to cut the stronghold off from the outside world and to protect his troops by building provisional ramparts and dams in the river. After that, trenches were dug closer and closer to the fortress. From these trenches the bastions were harassed with gunfire until the defense was breached. Through these breaches the stronghold could then be assailed.
1. the besieged stronghold; 2. assailed bastion; 3. trenches with artillery and zigzag connections; 4. provisional ramparts with encampments of the besiegers; 5. dams in the river; 6. food and artillery supplies.

The city in the background of this painting is Breda, surrounded by a maze of fortifications. During the siege of 1624-1625, both the Dutch and the Spanish armies dug trenches and built defenses. The Dutch also built dams and dykes to flood the surrounding fields. In return, the Spanish constructed an ingenious network of canals to siphon off the water around the city. 'Isabella visiting the encampment near Breda' is a painting by P. Snaeyers.

The siege of 's-Hertogenbosch in 1629, seen from the Dutch encampment. In the background the fortifications can be seen. Contemporary painting by Palames Palamedesz.

developments in fortification technology. The housing, created according to a pleasant and well-planned design, has been attributed to the civil architect Vincenzo Scamozzi, whose ideas probably influenced Marcantonio Barbaro, a politician and administrator of the Republic with humanist ideals and connoisseur of Renaissance ideas on the *ideal city*. The most important contributor was Giulio Savorgnan, a politician, military officer, self-styled engineer, one of Venice's most prominent experts in fortification, who had directed and inspired the Republic's previous defense plans. What was the result of all these disparate and not always harmonious contributions? In terms of town planning, Palmanova seems to be a compromise – albeit a happy one – between military needs and the requirements of civilian life. The new city, which has a nine-sided polygonal perimeter, a central hexagonal piazza and a radial form, seemed to people of the time to be the ideal, if abstract, realization of new fortification techniques, and its impressive geometry was successful because it harked back to the medieval symbolism of the circular city. Palmanova became a model city-fortress, was copied by engineers such as Perret and Specklin and was reproduced in innumerable cosmographies and treatises.

In functional and political terms, however, Palmanova was a failure; and this became clear even in the early stages of construction. The fragmentation of responsibilities caused constant confusion, corruption took place, delays built up which made costs soar. The working conditions were harsh, many of the 7,000 workers called up from the surrounding areas fled and the work cost many lives. The quality of labor was poor and the designers were forced to modify and simplify the original instructions. When completed, Palmanova acted as the bulwark of Venice during the

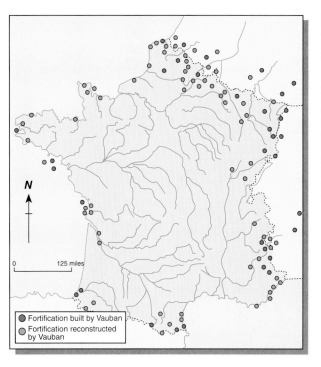

French defenses, built or rebuilt by Vauban (drawing after J. Verroust). Because of the system of fortifications along the borders, the country seems to be a fortified stronghold itself.

Gradisca war (1615), but as a settlement it was condemned from the outset to a hard life. Despite its efforts, the Venetian Republic was unable to attract people to a poor, uninhabited and insalubrious area. Not even Napoleon's attempts two centuries later succeeded in transforming this abstract container into a real city. Nowadays, the geometrical dimensions of Palmanova have virtually disappeared, and are visible only from the air.

Costs and ambitions

Like Palmanova, many ambitious plans were drawn up in the sixteenth century which later had to be

Louis XIV of France visiting his troops in the trenches of Tournai in 1667. Detail of a painting by Robert Bonnart.

The French cavalry encampment during the siege of Maastricht in 1673. Two horses have been stalled in front of every tent. In the middle the fodder supplies. Detail of a 17th century painting.

Mont-Louis, a small town in the French Pyrenees and a forward position of strategic importance in the wars with Spain, was strengthened with a huge citadel between 1679 and 1691. Town and citadel were surrounded by a second line of defense as well.

commitments, the Habsburg Empire itself did not have the necessary resources to implement a complete revision of existing permanent fortifications, other than in limited areas. In the Iberian peninsula (and in the British Isles) the *trace italienne* arrived quite late. Responsibility for the defense of the Spanish Empire was left mainly to the armies and fleets. On the whole, the progress of fortifications was faster than economic and social development in Europe and the financial resources of the various states were thus insufficient to meet such enormous commitments.

Apart from the exorbitant costs, another negative aspect of 'modern' fortification was its traumatic impact on the landscape and urban structure of the city. The gigantic fortifications and the geometrical rigor of their path were, in themselves, abstract and anti-historical elements, but the most serious damage was caused by the knocking down of entire suburbs, churches, monasteries, villas and gardens, trees and all kinds of vegetation in a vast area around the fortress.

In some cases, the construction of an urban fortress – such as the *Fortezza da Basso* in Florence and the *Rocca Paolina* built by Pope Paul III in Perugia – was the manifestation of a tyrannical government. Citadels and bastions complied with the wishes of princes, the building sites fuelled corruption and the cities watched powerless while highly expensive structures were built without their consent. The citadels required by the tyrannical governments were designed to meet a dual function: firstly to shelter the armed forces and secondly to provide a refuge for the dominant faction in the event of a revolt. In order to mask these needs, the governments sometimes commissioned monuments or decorative elements to counterbalance the impact of the fortress, or they appealed to municipal pride by presenting the fortification as an asset to the city.

scaled down. Military architects tried to reproduce the ideas of the treatises in reality, and did not always take into account the requirements of their clients, the real abilities of the labor force, and the restrictions imposed by cost and the irregular flow of financing. It was not only cities and small states which found it hard to provide the financial means needed for large-scale fortification programs. Around the middle of the sixteenth century, because of military ambitions and

Sieges and garrisons

The revolution in the methods of fortification was accompanied by new methods of siege. In the fifteenth century, the besiegers approached the walls of the fortress and used bombards to create a breach in a vulnerable section of the wall. This was followed by a mass assault which was usually conclusive. From the middle of the sixteenth century, the conquest of a fortress defended according to the principles of the *trace italienne* required counter-fortification work and much longer and laborious approach methods. The Spanish siege of Breda, in the Netherlands, involved surrounding the city with a double row of fortifications, defended from the inside and from the outside by 96 redoubts, 37 forts and 45 batteries. As in the Middle Ages, however, fortresses were often conquered without bombardment. Breda gave up through hunger after a nine month siege, without a single cannon being used against its bastions. In 1585, Antwerp suffered the same fate after a fifteen month siege, isolated by flooding of the surrounding plains.

Sieges often involved the deployment of thousands of men. When the Dutch attacked the fortress of 's-Hertogenbosch, they deployed 25,000 men to form a 40-kilometer (24-mile) long curtain right around the stronghold. In 1683, the Christian army defeated the Ottomans who were besieging Vienna because the enemy had pointed all its cannons at the city and had not bothered to build a rear line of defense to form a barrier against a rescuing army.

The features of bastioned defenses and the improvement of siege techniques led to important changes being brought to the conduct of war. War turned into an endless series of sieges, and the significant increase in the size of armies – which was the most significant development of the 'military revolution' – was largely absorbed by siege operations and by the defense of fortresses and cities. It has been calculated that in 1639 almost half of the 77,000 men who made up the Spanish army in Flanders were posted in fortresses, while the army of the United Provinces was deployed in garrisons which were often far more numerous than the civilian population they were defending. In 1632, in the campaign in which he lost his life, Gustavus Adolphus led 183,000 soldiers in Europe; of these only 20,000 actually fought with him, another part was made up of independent regional forces and the main body was stationed in fortresses and garrisons. In the first years of bastioned fortification, the states had deluded themselves into thinking they would save on the cost of garrisons, but it soon became clear that the more up-to-date and sophisticated the fortress, the more men were needed to defend and run it.

In the seventeenth century the great spread of bastioned fortification encouraged the setting up of national schools in France, Germany and the Netherlands. Among the most prominent technical exponents of the field in northern Europe one should mention the Alsatian engineer Daniel Specklin (his treatise *Architectura von Vestungen*, which was full of innova-

tive ideas, was published in Strasbourg in 1589) and Simon Stevin, a native of Bruges, who was a mathematical theorist, expert in hydraulics and siege techniques and military adviser to Maurice of Nassau. Despite the influences of the *trace italienne*, the technical innovations introduced by the Dutch school, and more generally the northern school, modified the technique of fortification and revolutionized methods of siege. As illustrated by the example of Coevorden, rebuilt by Maurice of Nassau after he conquered it from the Spaniards in 1592, the principal element of the fortified perimeter was no longer the bastion, but the advanced, highly elaborate and developed work carried out both outside and inside. Compared to the

FIGURE 1.

Fortifications demanded huge investments in infrastructure. Here, land surveyors of the French *Génie* (Corps of Engineers) are tracing out and marking the foundations, while masons are working higher up. Colored drawing from the 'Atlas' by Masse, an engineer-topographer and assistant on Vauban's staff.

classical Italian fortifications the new fortresses had a far more aggressive and dynamic profile. The northern school followed rigorously scientific concepts and an important part of construction was a thorough survey of the land. At the end of the seventeenth century, the Dutchmen Henrik Ruse and Menno van Coehoorn introduced some very important innovations which represented an improvement on local techniques. The publication of treatises also flourished in France in line with a current review of defensive structures. At the time of Richelieu and Louis XIII, the permanent defenses of France underwent selective restructuring work. Among the most prominent treatises are those of the engineers employed by the Engineering Corps set up by Sully, such as Errard de Bar-le Duc and Blaise de Pagan.

Vauban

The second half of the seventeenth century was characterized by the life and exceptional works, by their size and excellence of design, of Sebastien Le Prestre, Marquis of Vauban, in the service of the hegemonical plans of the France of Louis XIV and his ministers.
The most important period of Vauban's career began in 1667, when Louis XIV acquired a number of important cities in Flanders. Continuing the work of his predecessors, Vauban aimed to pare down and rationalize a system of defense which was too costly and obsolete, and attempted to provide France with a frontier which would not only be easy to defend, but would also allow further conquest, in line with the king's expansionist policies. Under his guidance, and often on the basis of his plans, French engineers built and rebuilt strongholds, creating a string of powerful defenses along the frontiers. The central areas of France were, to all intents and purposes, demilitarized, thus making large numbers of men available taken from the garrisons. The most innovative work carried out by Vauban was the city-fortress of Neuf-Brisach, built between 1698 and 1706 to defend the crossings over the Rhine from the Swiss side. The bastions have almost disappeared while the forward external structures are large and confer a highly aggressive character on the perimeter of the fortress.

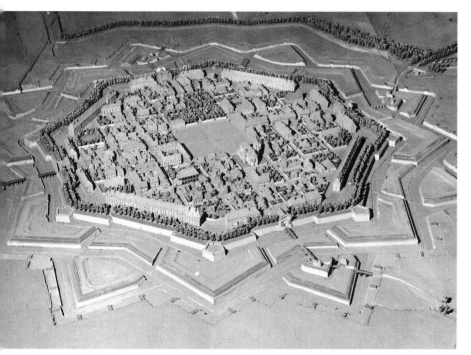

Scale model of the strongly fortified garrison town of Neuf-Brisach, situated at 1.2 miles from the river Rhine, where 4,000 troops were quartered. The construction of the defenses lasted from 1669 until 1712.

Vauban's fame among his contemporaries was particularly the result of his innovations in siege techniques. In 1673 in Maastricht he first tested a system of progressive approach by parallel trenches. With long preparatory work, the pioneers traced a network of excavations aimed at bringing the besieger closer and closer to the fortress, and shelters and defenses were built to protect during counterattacks. Numerous editions were published of Vauban's treatise on sieges, written in 1705 for the Duke of Bourgogne, and it became an important work of technical and cultural reference for eighteenth century engineers.
With Coehoorn and Vauban, military architecture acquired systematic scientific foundations and methods of procedure which involved the mechanical application of repetitive forms and procedures: the time of experiments and great innovations essentially came to an end with the close of the seventeenth century.

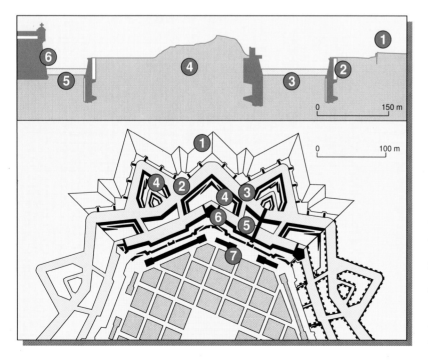

Cross-section and ground plan of Vauban's fortifications in Neuf-Brisach. In order to offer better resistance to gunfire, Vauban made ramparts out of earth which could not be breached by cannonballs. In the moats surrounding the stronghold, lunetees and ravelins were constructed: extended half-moon-shaped fortifications making the enemy's approach to the city walls as difficult as possible. 1. glacis (field of fire) with first parapet; 2. covered corridor; 3. outer moat; 4. lunetees and ravelins; 5. city moat; 6. bastion and city walls; 7. barracks and buildings within the city.

Emilio Busi painted 'Liberty guiding the people' during the heyday of the *Risorgimento* movement which led to the unification of Italy (1820-1861). It is a heroical evocation of the Genoese popular rising against the Austrians.

Collective violence in early modern Europe

The sixteenth and seventeenth centuries brought Europe into a vigorous, violent age of revolution. The transformations of commercial and political organization in early modern Europe altered the lives of most Europeans and stimulated and channelled Europe's collective violence. Although revolutionary situations varied enormously from region to region and group to group, they sprang up all over the continent.

Charles Tilly

In 1780 the fanatical Protestant Lord George Gordon called for an armed revolt against cheap Irish laborers, resulting in violent riots in London. These 'Gordon Riots' were the most bloody and destructive of the 18th century. Contemporary popular print.

On November 9, 1747, a discontented crowd rammed open the door of the office of the mayor of Amsterdam. The rising was a protest against the authorities' failure to reform the system of government. Painting by Reinier Vinkeles (1786).

The forms of early modern revolution, it is true, did not generally resemble those a later era came to regard as truly revolutionary: the seizure of state power from unjust rulers by a newly mobilized social class that had long endured oppression. Instead, the early modern period's revolutions ranged from enormous struggles over religious doctrine to resistance against aggressively expanding monarchies to civil wars aligning partisans of rival claimants for royal power. Yet they were all revolutionary in the sense that they involved fractionation of previously coherent political power, implied new relations between rulers and ruled and sometimes produced substantial shifts in who ruled and how. Revolutionary situations sprang up from one end of Europe to the other because the articulation between everyday social routines and forms of government was changing rapidly under the influence of new connections between Europe and other parts of the world.

For two millennia before 1500, Europe had operated as a northwestern appendage of the world's greatest system of political economy, the huge band of trade and conquest extending from what parochial Europeans now call the Middle East out to the Far East and thence to the Pacific. One of the system's major extensions reached north across Mongol territory through Muscovy to Scandinavia, while another ran from the eastern Mediterranean up the Adriatic, across the Alps, down the Rhine to the North Sea and a third passed through mainly Muslim lands and seas into

Iberia. Only during the fifteenth century did these tentacles of the vast Eurasian octopus begin to swell, merge and play a dominant part in the entire system's life. Iberian and Dutch ventures into the Atlantic and Indian Oceans gave Europeans a significant share of long-distance trade and established a flow of American silver through Europe all the way to China. In the process, the population grew rapidly throughout Eurasia, including mainland Europe. Even then Ottoman, Persian and other Muslim Empires blocked the most direct paths between Europe and the world's richest regions, while further east fragments and successors of the once-enormous Mongol Empire still controlled much of the precious overland route to China.

These changes underlay a significant expansion of both political and mercantile power in Europe. The continent underwent a 'military revolution' including increased use of artillery, the development of siege tactics, bulky fortifications and massed mercenary infantry. It also saw an eventual movement towards standing armies recruited from the national population and paid for by rapidly rising taxation as well as augmented engagement of Atlantic powers' navies in both commerce and warfare throughout the world. Such transformations of commercial and political organization altered the lives of most Europeans, although in greatly variable ways depending on the region and state. In this way they stimulated and channelled Europe's revolutionary situations.

Claim-making repertoires

At a level short of revolution, violent conflict likewise flourished because of contradictions between forms of rule and conditions of routine social life. Collective violence follows a paradoxical order, depending heavily on the routines by which people assemble, communicate, make claims and counter claims other people are making. Claim-making routines range from the intrinsically violent (e.g. attempted assassination) to the only contingently violent (e.g. mass meetings, which rarely produce physical violence except when authorities or rivals seek to disrupt them). Any particular population knows only a limited number of routines for making claims – a 'claim-making repertoire' –

An infuriated crowd looting the house of A.M. van Aarsen, a hated tax collector in Amsterdam. Drawing from 1777 by Simon Fokke.

In 1789 the plight of the poor, devoid of any political influence, became pressing as never before due to steep rises in the prices of basic foodstuffs. On the morning of July 14, 1789, an unstoppable crowd marched on the arsenal of Paris and looted guns and rifles. The following assault and capture of the *Bastille*, the royal prison, was an event of which the symbolic significance cannot be overstated. Its demolition meant the victory of the people over the king.

The hated ring of toll bars around Paris had been conceived and supervised by the architect Nicolas Ledoux (1736-1806). At the outbreak of the Revolution these toll bars and their tax collectors were among the first victims of the popular fury.

Women more than held their own in revolutions. Here Parisian market women, carrying stabbing weapons and a gun, are marching on the Royal palace at Versailles. In 1793 many women united themselves in the 'Association of revolutionary republican women' (which soon became defunct). Drawing by an anonymous artist.

as a function of its social organization, its relations to other groups and the history of its previous struggles. Claim-making repertoires strongly constrain the form and incidence of collective violence. In sixteenth and seventeenth century Europe, people knew how to assemble and deliberately rarely knew how to conduct blood feuds, while journeymen who attacked each other (verbally or otherwise) under the cover of Mardi Gras rarely banded together to tear down fences around recently enclosed land.

The precise forms of collective violence thus varied enormously from region to region and group to group because they depended intimately on the highly variable texture of power and social relations; clan-divided rural Ireland differed greatly from intensely commercialized urban Holland, which in turn differed fundamentally from landlord-dominated Poland and the Ottoman vassal states of the Balkans. Violent struggles over the marketing of food, for example, became frequent in England during the sixteenth century, while in France they only multiplied at the end of the seventeenth. The difference depended, among other things, on the timing, pace and form of agricultural commercialization in the two countries. Similarly, rivalries among local lineages continued to incite violent struggles in Ireland, the Balkans and Corsica long after they had ceased to figure significantly in Germany or Scandinavia. Since most important conflicts sometimes generated attacks on persons or objects, to trace the history of collective violence is to follow the fluctuations of popular struggle in general.

Regional differences did not fall into a linear progression from 'backward' to 'advanced' forms of conflict; they endured as a function of contrasting principles of social organization. In the Low Countries, for instance, urban rebellions dominated the sixteenth century's large-scale violence because ambitious princes repeatedly sought to extend their control over the wealth and

Against all odds the civilian militia and the people of Flanders succeeded in repelling the Dutch army, turning the Belgian Revolution of 1830 into a success. Detail of an impression drawn by F.J. Navez.

power of mercantile municipalities. Leaders of wealthy, autonomous cities could mobilize resistance based on rich internal organization and broad external contacts. Meanwhile, in Poland armed struggles of nobles and their clientele to seize control of the crown or to assure their own autonomy racked the countryside, directly reflecting the segmentation of both economy and policy into patron-client chains of noble landlords who controlled private armies. The capital-wielding Low Countries produced distinctly different patterns of collective violence from coercive Poland.

The variation extended to such ostensibly non-political struggles as the Protestant Reformation. Almost all of Catholic Europe except Italy and Iberia hosted strong Protestant movements during the sixteenth century, although in such regions as Poland, Austria and France the Catholic Church eventually recovered most of its lost ground. Everywhere the local combination of popular enthusiasm, bourgeois alliance and princely response strongly affected the depth and durability of religious reform. On the whole Protestantism gained a more durable hold where sovereignty was fragmented, cities strong and noble landlords relatively unimportant. But there the variation began. In the zone we now call Switzerland and nearby German-speaking areas whole peasant communities allied with small-town workers to raise rebellions against their lords in the name of godliness. In France, Calvinist cells formed chiefly among urban merchants and craftsmen, who engaged in violent struggle mainly in local rivalries with committed Catholics or in reaction to royal attempts to suppress their cult.

In England, Tudor monarchs repeatedly attempted top-down religious organization only to encounter popular resistance. That resistance ranged from local attacks on royalist clergy to the vast Pilgrimage of Grace (1536-1537), which arose when Henry VIII seized the Catholic monasteries and their wealth in the name of a new state church. Even within the small compass of the Low Countries the form and fate of Protestantism varied, fitting snugly into the prosperous, autonomous municipalities of the north, pitting popular enthusiasts against powerful landlords and

This giant 'liberty hat' was put on top of the Tree of Liberty in 1795 on the main square in Haarlem (the Netherlands) after the revolution incited by revolutionary pro-French 'patriotists' and 'liberators'.

Student revolutionaries discussing the situation in the guards' room of the Vienna University auditorium during the Revolution of 1848. Students have, by their actions, often forced the speed of shifting political attitudes among other intellectual groups.

Swiss mercenaries

Just outside the city gates of Lucerne is the 'dying lion of Lucerne', a monument hewn out of sandstone by Lukas Ahorn to commemorate the courage of the Swiss Guards of Louis XVI who were defeated near the Tuileries in 1792. They were not the first paid Swiss soldiers to die far from home.

Mercenaries are professional soldiers who do not fight for their political convictions or because they have been conscripted, but for money. From the time of the earliest wars onwards (Egypt, Mesopotamia) to the development of national standing armies (mid-seventeenth century), state troops were frequently reinforced with mercenaries. Often they were foreigners; the Roman emperors had a German Guard and the English king, Harold, used Danes to defeat Norway. Great empires, it seemed, could often not be built and maintained with (local) militia; armies of mercenaries were the power instruments of the absolute thriving state.

After the Hundred Years' War (1337-1453) Europe was overrun with thousands of men whose only training was in fighting. During the fifteenth century 'free companies' of Swiss, Italian and German soldiers roamed through Europe and sold their services to local rulers, their loyalty dependent on the payment received. Hirelings were directly recruited from densely populated countries with a military tradition. The Swiss, in particular, were famed as the best soldiers of Europe, especially after the battle at St. Jakob an der Birs

(1444) when 1,500 Swiss fended off an army of 40,000 French led by Louis XI. In the centuries to follow, France, Italy, the Vatican and many others fought to acquire these Swiss military services. In the Alpine cantons this led to depopulation, discord about the distribution of the spoils of war, corruption and bitterness. On the other hand, the French religious wars and the Thirty Years' War formed an outlet for overpopulation, provided much work opportunity and the neutrality of Switzerland itself was guaranteed by agreements with all the warring parties.

In May 1521 the Swiss cantons formed an alliance with France, in which in return for annual payment, soldiers were placed at the disposal of the French king and assured him of extra support in cases of emergency. Eventually, in the period of Louis XI to XIV (1465-1715) more than a million Swiss served at the French court. In 1616 by Royal Decree their regiment became a guard. A similar military body-

Both the *Bastille* in 1792 and the Louvre palace in 1830 were guarded by well-drilled Swiss soldiers when they were assaulted by armed revolutionaries. Here the violent clash between revolutionaries and the Swiss guards in the courtyard of the Louvre (July 29, 1830) which ended the rule of King Charles X. Detail of a painting by Jean Louis Bézard (1832).

guard, the *Guardia Svizzera*, served the popes from the fifteenth century (and continuously from 1505) onwards right up to the present day.

It was only after the French Revolution that the Swiss cantons stopped publicly renting out their citizens, and in 1859 the Confederation forbade recruitment to foreign armies.

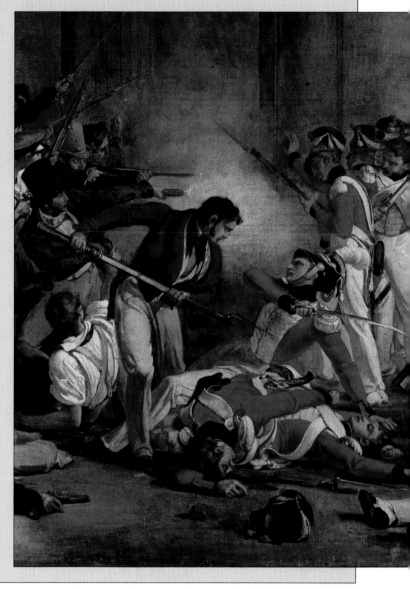

Nevertheless, Swiss mercenaries continued to form part of the European forces. Napoleon acquired the rights to a contingent of 16,000 Swiss and in the Crimean War, beside 10,000 Germans and 5,000 Italians, 5,000 Swiss also fought on the British side. Money and neutrality once again proved more important than politics.

---

churchmen in the south. Despite widespread attacks on Catholic images, objects and places of worship in Flanders during the 1560s, and despite the declared adherence of nearly one third of the urban population to the various Protestant denominations, the military overweight of Habsburg Spain forced those segments of the population back to Catholicism or to emigrate, thus contributing massively to the success of Calvinism in Holland.

Monarchs and peoples

Similarly, the military revolution had different effects depending on the social environment. Most states

turned to the massive hiring of mercenaries, which immediately put their population and their enemies at risk of rape, pillage and hostage taking, not to mention mutinies when the troops' pay arrived too late.

Sweden, however, tried to minimize its reliance on mercenaries by building a domestic army of peasant-soldiers coupled with a vast system of priestly and bureaucratic control. Resistance to that system's implantation generated distinctive forms of collective violence. In expansive Moscovy, the lines between war, revolution and smaller-scale collective violence blurred badly, but rulers from Ivan the Great (1462-1505) onwards built a patrimonial system in which

The *sansculotte* dress of popular combatants during the French Revolution (1792), painted by L.L. Boilly.

nobles and office holders held enormous political and economic power in their own domains on condition of supplying revenues, military force and loyalty to the czar. The increasingly subjugated peasants, who paid the patrimonial system's major costs, rebelled repeatedly (if, on the whole, unsuccessfully) as that system formed. The move to mass armies had profoundly variable effects as a function of regional social organization and therefore generated very different sorts of collective violence among the diverse European regions.

Consider contrasts between the British Isles and France. During the years 1500-1700 revolutionary situations – struggles in which power over a state split into at least two segments for a month or more – appeared in 76 of the British Isles' years and 70 of France's years, roughly one year in three. Because of fragmented and contested sovereignty, it is harder to distinguish war from revolution in the British Isles. Eighteenth century Scots and Irishmen often claimed, after all, they were not rebelling against 'their' monarch but against an alien imperial power; what is

A Tuscan volunteer in the *Risorgimento* army, portrayed by A. Puccinelli (1848).

An armed man of the people, Vienna, 1848.

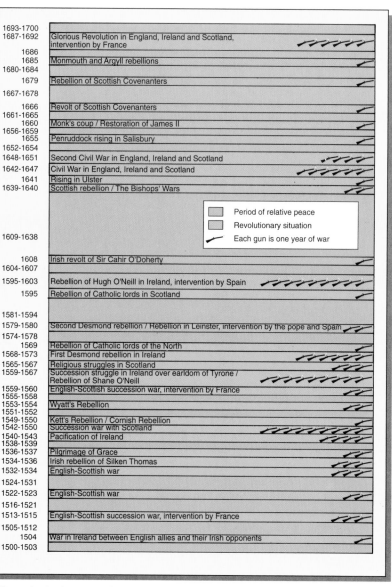

1693-1700		
1687-1692	Glorious Revolution in England, Ireland and Scotland, intervention by France	✎✎✎✎✎✎
1686		
1685	Monmouth and Argyll rebellions	✎
1680-1684		
1679	Rebellion of Scottish Covenanters	✎
1667-1678		
1666	Revolt of Scottish Covenanters	✎
1661-1665		
1660	Monk's coup / Restoration of James II	✎
1656-1659		
1655	Penruddock rising in Salisbury	✎
1652-1654		
1648-1651	Second Civil War in England, Ireland and Scotland	✎✎✎✎
1642-1647	Civil War in England, Ireland and Scotland	✎✎✎✎✎✎
1641	Rising in Ulster	✎
1639-1640	Scottish rebellion / The Bishops' Wars	✎✎
1609-1638		
1608	Irish revolt of Sir Cahir O'Doherty	✎
1604-1607		
1595-1603	Rebellion of Hugh O'Neill in Ireland, intervention by Spain	✎✎✎✎✎✎✎✎✎
1595	Rebellion of Catholic lords in Scotland	✎
1581-1594		
1579-1580	Second Desmond rebellion / Rebellion in Leinster, intervention by the pope and Spain	✎✎
1574-1578		
1569	Rebellion of Catholic lords of the North	✎
1568-1573	First Desmond rebellion in Ireland	✎✎✎✎✎
1565-1567	Religious struggles in Scotland	✎✎✎
1559-1567	Succession struggle in Ireland over earldom of Tyrone / Rebellion of Shane O'Neill	✎✎✎✎✎✎✎✎
1559-1560	English-Scottish succession war, intervention by France	✎✎
1555-1558		
1553-1554	Wyatt's Rebellion	✎✎
1551-1552		
1549-1550	Kett's Rebellion / Cornish Rebellion	✎✎✎✎✎✎✎
1542-1550	Succession war with Scotland	
1540-1543	Pacification of Ireland	✎✎✎✎
1538-1539		
1536-1537	Pilgrimage of Grace	✎✎
1534-1536	Irish rebellion of Silken Thomas	✎✎✎
1532-1534	English-Scottish war	✎✎✎
1524-1531		
1522-1523	English-Scottish war	✎✎
1516-1521		
1513-1515	English-Scottish succession war, intervention by France	✎✎✎
1505-1512		
1504	War in Ireland between English allies and their Irish opponents	✎
1500-1503		

Legend:
- Period of relative peace
- Revolutionary situation
- Each gun is one year of war

Chronological survey of the inland uprisings in the British Isles between 1500 and 1700.

History shows that once a revolutionary movement has come to power, it is often short of qualified people to fill all government positions with people from its own ranks. This strengthens counter-revolutionary tendencies and sometimes, as in France, ends in the restoration of the old regime, leading to another revolution. Here a crowd is burning the royal throne at the base of the Column of Liberty in Paris in 1848.

more, France repeatedly aligned itself with Scottish or Irish rebels. But even in France the end of the religious wars with Henry VI's accession (1598) left a number of Protestant cities in protected, contingent relations with the crown, a condition Henry's successors fought zealously (and at last successfully) to eliminate. In short, the forms of revolution reflected the forms of state power.

In both Britain and France, the sixteenth and seventeenth centuries brought momentous transformations of state power. As of 1500, at least three distinct policies, those of England, Scotland and Ireland, coexisted in the British Isles. Henry VII had emerged from fifteenth century English civil wars and struggles with France to become the first Tudor king. His successors, including Henry VIII and Elizabeth I, consolidated royal power in pursuit not only of mastery over their domestic rivals but also control over wars with Spain and France. Starting with Henry VIII's top-down Reformation (1534), most of them also worked at subordinating ecclesiastical wealth and power to the crown. Their increasing reliance on public taxation rather than private revenues (the distinction itself was sharpening) likewise strengthened Parliament. In Scotland, the Stuart clan held nominal rule with intermittent French support but under increasing threat of English control. In Ireland, finally, an English viceroy contended with virtually autonomous regional warlords. Nevertheless, the politics of the three lands intersected incessantly, enough so that it makes some sense to treat them as a single loosely articulated political entity.

The succession of James Stuart to the English crown in 1603 (itself the long-distance consequence of the standard European aristocratic propensity for defensive dynastic alliances, which produced frequent Scots-English intermarriages) connected the two kingdoms more firmly, but also initiated a series of struggles between the crown, Parliament and great mag-

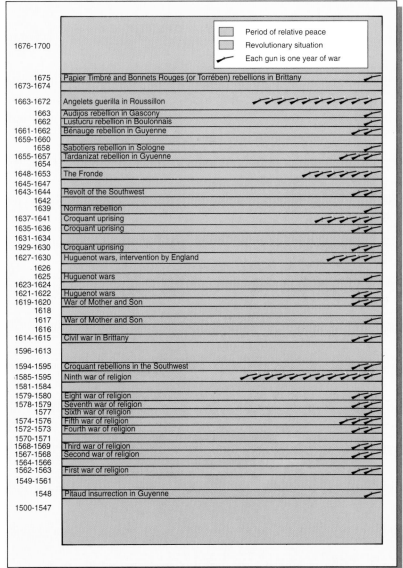

	Period of relative peace
	Revolutionary situation
	Each gun is one year of war

1676-1700	
1675	Papier Timbré and Bonnets Rouges (or Torrében) rebellions in Brittany
1673-1674	
1663-1672	Angelets guerilla in Roussillon
1663	Audijos rebellion in Gascony
1662	Lustucru rebellion in Boulonnais
1661-1662	Bénauge rebellion in Guyenne
1659-1660	
1658	Sabotiers rebellion in Sologne
1655-1657	Tardanizat rebellion in Gyuenne
1654	
1648-1653	The Fronde
1645-1647	
1643-1644	Revolt of the Southwest
1642	
1639	Norman rebellion
1637-1641	Croquant uprising
1635-1636	Croquant uprising
1631-1634	
1929-1630	Croquant uprising
1627-1630	Huguenot wars, intervention by England
1626	
1625	Huguenot wars
1623-1624	
1621-1622	Huguenot wars
1619-1620	War of Mother and Son
1618	
1617	War of Mother and Son
1616	
1614-1615	Civil war in Brittany
1596-1613	
1594-1595	Croquant rebellions in the Southwest
1585-1595	Ninth war of religion
1581-1584	
1579-1580	Eight war of religion
1578-1579	Seventh war of religion
1577	Sixth war of religion
1574-1576	Fifth war of religion
1572-1573	Fourth war of religion
1570-1571	
1568-1569	Third war of religion
1567-1568	Second war of religion
1564-1566	
1562-1563	First war of religion
1549-1561	
1548	Pitaud insurrection in Guyenne
1500-1547	

Chronological survey of the inland uprisings in France between 1500 and 1700

When the French army, assisted by German troops, crushed the Commune of Paris in May 1871, 17,000 *communards* or revolutionaries were killed in one week.

nates that eventually broke into the civil war (1642-1647), led to the execution of King Charles I (1649), a new civil war (1648-1651), establishment of a revolutionary government (1651-1660), restoration of the monarchy (1660), yet another civil war (1687-1692) and the creation of a new regime in which both Parliament and a state church shared greatly augmented power with the monarch.

In France, likewise, sixteenth and seventeenth century political change produced an almost unrecognizably different regime by the death of Louis XIV in 1714. As of 1500, France had finally incorporated Brittany after a century of struggle, and was undertaking a major military rivalry with Spain in Italy and at sea. As elsewhere in Europe, the successful pursuit of war augmented the state's domestic power while leaving the state more vulnerable to resistance on the part of those who paid the military bills. In France, however, bloody civil wars in which dynastic, family alliance and religious divisions interlocked wracked the country repeatedly between the 1560s and 1620s. Not until the early eighteenth century, indeed, did Louis XIV put down France's last great popular religious rebellion, that of the Camisards. The extension of royal power under Henry IV, Louis XIII and Louis XIV (accelerated by the grand reentry of France into

It was not unusual for the authorities, whose very officials belonged to the propertied classes, to send in the armed forces to crush workers' revolts. Drawing depicting the 'Peterloo Massacre' of 1819 in Manchester.

In highly industrialized countries, such as Great Britain and Belgium, strikes for higher wages and better working conditions were a recurrent phenomenon throughout the 19th century. This engraving shows John Burns addressing the men on strike at the gates of the London Docks in 1889.

Europe's general wars after 1630) engaged the whole country in repeated struggles, but resulted in co-optation of previously autonomous lords, courts and regional assemblies.

Patterns

These political histories entailed characteristically different patterns of revolution and collective violence in Britain and France. In the early modern British Isles, revolutionary situations sprang chiefly from actions directly concerning the crown: state-initiated religious innovations, enlarged royal claims for service or revenues, succession struggles when the heir-apparent was a child, an unmarried woman or a Catholic. Such events distinguished themselves from everyday and local violence. Forcible seizures of grain in times of shortage and high prices, struggles among rival groups of workers and collective opposition to cutting forests, drainage of marshes and enclosure of commons or wastelands predominated at the smaller scale. As compared with struggles over food or enclosures, revolution-generating events typically affected many groups and large areas of Britain simultaneously, bore directly on the state, engaged important public identities or factions and involved some great autonomous power holders.

While the same generalizations hold for France, the resulting pattern of collective violence came out rather differently because of contrasting social and political conditions. Although the France of 1500 wielded immense economic power by comparison with upstarts England, Scotland and Ireland, the British economy already enjoyed a favored connection with the Low Countries, extensive maritime experience and, not least, a protected military position. France's economic, social and political life depended even more heavily than Britain's on great landlords who had accumulated or retained substantial political powers. Furthermore, within limits set by powerful lords, French peasants had established much stronger claims on land and local administration than their British (and especially their English) counterparts. The division sharpened between 1500 and 1700, as the British population, both rural and urban, proletarianized much more rapidly than the French. But throughout the period French peasants, landlords, artisans and bourgeoisie all confronted a relatively unitary state with established rights and claims of their own.

In that setting, struggles over food supply, rights to common land workers' corporate privileges and public morality certainly recurred, producing their share

The weeks preceding the Russian Revolution of October 1917 saw a deluge of inflammatory speeches and demonstrations. Lenin addressed protesting factory workers in St. Petersburg, where the first 'Red Guard' units were established. Painting by A. Serov.

Rosa Luxemburg was one of the protagonists of the so-called 'betrayed' German 'Spartacus' revolution of 1918-1919. She was arrested and murdered on January 15, 1919, two months after the proclamation of the Socialist Republic.

of collective violence. On a larger scale, however, three interlocking forms of conflict produced the major bursts of violence. The first was the enmity of Protestants and Catholics, which ran from local vandalism of each other's sanctuaries to the civil wars that tore the entire country apart between 1562 and 1598, only to recur regionally through the early eighteenth century. Until Louis XIV finally killed, exiled or converted most of their lordly leaders, large-scale Protestant actions usually stemmed from coalitions between urban artisans and merchants on one side and dissident aristocrats on the other.

The second predominant form of violent conflict in sixteenth and seventeenth century France was wholesale resistance to government attempts to extract new revenue for its military efforts. Greatly augmented taxes and removals of fiscal exemptions typically involved questions of justice, since they violated well-established treaties between crown and localities, gave a royal agent or contractor extraordinary powers and privileges or seized the property of chartered institutions (especially guilds and municipalities) without compensation or due process. Ordinary people responded by attacking tax collectors, destroying symbols of royal authority, refusing payment, driving out new office holders or joining armed rebellions – the latter almost always in alliance with regional magnates, and usually under the direction of military veterans. As France continued its great wars with Spain between 1514 and 1551, for example, serious tax rebellions took place in the cities of Agen, Bordeaux, La Rochelle, St. Maixent, Sarlat, Niort, Saintes, Périgueux, St. Foy and a number of southern regions. During Louis XIV's great seventeenth century wars, the rebellions of the Tardanizats, Sabotiers, Bénauge, Lustucru, Audijos, Angelets, Papier Timbré, Bonnets Rouges and Torrében all responded in part to physical pressure, although by that time grandees were disappearing from France's full-scale rebellions.

The third category includes dynastic struggles, involving the clients of rival claimants to royal power, including the existing king or queen. The two wars between factions of Maria de'Medici and her son Louis XIII (1617-1620) provide extreme examples. But until 1630 France's religious wars all combined dynastic with sectarian rivalries, and the larger tax rebellions generally drew on complicity or alliance with ambitious regional power holders. The culmination arrived with the Fronde (1648-1653), in which popular mobilization crystallized around fiscal and financial grievances, while would-be kings and king-makers such as the Prince of Condé and Cardinal Mazarin marched armies around the country and invaded Paris itself. The Fronde temporarily suspended the monarchy. Once Louis XIV, his mother Anne of Austria and Mazarin regained power, they concerted a campaign of administrative reorganization and repression that permanently changed the character of state power, neutralized the nobility as an autonomous political force and ironically gave a more popular cast to large rebellions than they had shown since the early sixteenth century.

Ornamental bowl with nautilus shell, which shows an engraving of an unspecified sea battle. The silver figure at the base is Munatius Plancus, the legendary founder of the city of Basel, dressed as a Roman general. Hans Jacob Birr commissioned Sebastian Fechter to make this elegant piece of art for the saffron guild in Basel in 1676.

Offstage in the wings

Europe's arsenals

They still capture the imagination: naval battles, waged by the floating castles of the seventeenth and eighteenth centuries. The power struggles between the mighty European states of the time have been depicted in a multitude of forms. Paintings, prints and drawings show us what it was like: spectacularly theatrical images in which enormous wooden warships play the leading role. But few realize what was happening offstage.

Els van Eijck van Heslinga

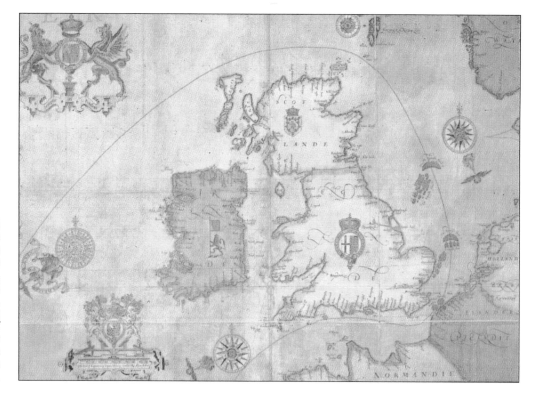

Map of the British Isles and the English Channel (1588), with the route followed by the Spanish Armada. At right, below, the Spanish and English fleets off Calais, where English fire ships inflicted heavy losses on the Armada. Pursued by the English, the Armada then set sail for the seas northwest of Scotland, where heavy summer storms sank a number of ships. Thence the remaining ships set off for an inglorious return to Spain.

In the second half of the sixteenth century most European lands went through an extensive organization of naval military might, though its form differed from country to country. In the Republic of the United Provinces of the Netherlands the navy consisted of five admiralties in the coastal provinces, each admiralty enjoying relative independence. In other European countries the navy was characterized by strong central organization. As an independent city-state Venice had built up its own marine forces many centuries before. But everywhere there were three recognizable elements which together formed the necessary basis for any successful navy in former times: a management structure, shipbuilding and/or repair facilities and supplies for the vessels.

Many sites in Europe still carry traces of this infrastructure. The remains of the office buildings that accommodated the officials, the wharves and docks for the construction and maintenance of the ships and the warehouses for the ships' supplies are today all being used for other purposes. But unlike the ships of the past the buildings are still tangibly present. It is quite feasible to do a round trip along the European coastline and visit all the sites of past major marine establishments or arsenals. The word 'arsenal', incidentally, has different interpretations in different places in Europe. In the southern countries and France it had a very wide meaning – a (military) complex of warehouses, other buildings, wharves and docks. Elsewhere in Europe an arsenal was simply the building where such things as weapons and ammunition were made or stored.

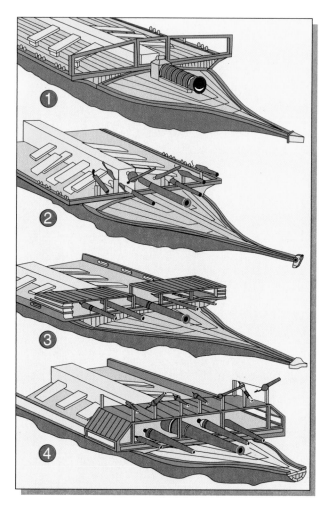

The use of artillery had a great influence on the building of warships. In a 100 years' time, the armament of the Mediterranean galleys was largely expanded. 1. Venetian galleon, c. 1486; 2. Genoan, Sicilian or Napolitan galleon, c. 1535; 3. Venetian galleon, c. 1571; 4. Spanish galleon, c. 1571. The abundant and clearly visible armament has made the battering ram superfluous.

The fleet of the Holy League, under the command of Don Juan, which joined battle with the Turks off Lepanto (Messina) in 1571, was made up of 208 galleys and 6 galleasses (merchant ships armed with guns). Venice contributed over half these ships. The fatal blow inflicted on the Ottoman fleet put an end to the Turkish raids on Mediterranean ships and ports.

Several European architects made a round trip of arsenals at the beginning of the nineteenth century. The route taken by one of them, the Italian engineer Andrea Salvini, went from Venice to Antwerp, Amsterdam and Hoorn and then southward to Ostend, Dunkirk, Dieppe, Le Havre, Cherbourg, St. Malo, Brest, Lorient, Nantes, Rochefort, Bordeaux, Bayonne and Marseilles. Doubtless the war situation was partly to blame for Santini not having gone further north to visit the English coast.

He could also have seen many interesting things in Spain and Portugal or, for that matter, on the island of Malta.

What Salvini saw, and what we can still see today, is that the design of the complexes and the architecture is very similar everywhere. Thought it is true to say that the buildings were erected with an eye to the local situation, it would seem that more or less the same requirements were imposed on the way in which the site was divided up and the warehouses distributed. Which, of course, had everything to do with the end-product: a successful fleet of fully equipped and manned wooden sailing ships.

Arsenals or navy establishments

The essential condition for the creation of a fleet of warships lies first and foremost in the need felt by a state to acquire power at sea as well as on land. Such a need can be based on politics or economics. The rise

Dutch sailors embarking on small riverboats, which will take them to their warships out in deeper water. Painting ascribed to Hendrik de Meijer, from the second half of the 17th century.

and fall of seafaring nations can be traced more or less exactly by noting the length of time the arsenals existed. Venice is a good example of a city-state which as early as at the start of the Middle Ages was able to equip many warships at one time when the occasion demanded. In the twelfth century, when the republic had established a solid position for itself both politically and economically, the decision was taken to build a single large central complex of wharves and

View of the arsenal shipbuilding yards in the harbor of Marseilles; a number of galleys are under construction. 17th century painting ascribed to Jean-Baptiste de la Roze.

The burning of the English fleet after the Dutch raid of June 20, 1667, at Chatham, the home base of the English fleet, was a psychological blow to the English. After the English ships had been rent apart by cannonballs, fireboats with burning pitch set the fleet ablaze.
Painting by Adriaen Pietersz. van de Venne.

docks. Known as the *Arsenale Vecchio*, it was extended further in the course of the centuries. The number of people employed there at any one time could be as high as fifteen thousand. Around 1600 Venice was capable of putting two hundred galleys to sea in a short time.

But the definitive fall of the republic in the eighteenth century also put an end to the glory of the Venetian arsenal. Other European countries had taken the lead. In the mid-seventeenth century larger naval complexes came into being in the Netherlands, followed shortly afterwards by England and France. In the second half of the eighteenth century the French minister Colbert took far-reaching measures designed to strengthen the arsenals of Toulon and Brest. It was even intended to build *'le plus grand et le plus beau (établissement) qu'il y ait dans le monde'* at Rochefort. In the northern part of Europe there followed Kronstadt in Russia, Sveaborg in Finland and Karlskrona in Sweden. In Spain, Cadiz and Cartagena were further developed. The arsenal of El Ferrol, at the northwestern tip of Spain, has a history typical of such places. Between 1750 and 1752 a gigantic complex was constructed, with a wharf containing seventeen docks and many stores. Thousands of people found employment there. But in 1825 the Dutch captain Maarten Schaap described El Ferrol as follows:

'Where once 5,000 to 7,000 people worked, now there is only grass. There were a few people there and a couple of guards. The stores were in a sorry state: empty, no timber or iron or hemp or ropes, no bitumen or tar to be seen. In a word, all the former glory of Spain was here transformed into misery'.

It was the nineteenth century that saw the last nail in the coffin of the arsenals, as described by Schaap. This had more to do with the development of the steam engine and the appearance of metal-hulled ships than with political factors. The building and maintenance of much larger iron vessels was radically different from the construction of relatively simple wooden sailing ships.

Management organization

The way the management of the battle fleets in Europe was organized varied greatly from country to country, depending on the type of state. Control in Venice was in the hands of a board, which was directly responsible to the Doge and his Great Council. Under the board there were two individuals with direct responsibility for managing the arsenal – a *Provveditore all' arsenale* and a *Provveditore all' artiglieri*, both of whom had experience of the field for which they held responsibility. The *Doge* came once a year to inspect the arsenal.

In the Republic of the Seven United Netherlands the organization of the navy was somewhat more complex. The large measure of independence enjoyed by the seven provinces made it impossible to have a single central navy. Five admiralties came into being in the three maritime provinces, that of Amsterdam being by far the largest.

Officially the Amsterdam admiralty was created in 1578, when the city allied itself with the Prince of Orange in the revolt against Spain. Amsterdam became one of the five seats of the Dutch navy, alongside Middelburg in Zeeland, Rotterdam, the Northern Quarter (Hoorn and Enkhuizen) and Dokkum (later Harlingen) in Friesland. Each admiralty was a self-contained unit, complete with wharf, warehouses and other facilities required to get ships into the water.

The main gateway into the Venetian Arsenal is a Renaissance-style triumphal arch (1460). The sculptures were only added in the 17th century. The bulwark however is of medieval gothic origin.

Sign (1753) of the cabinetmakers' guild of the Venetian Arsenal, representing a number of the guild's activities. The accompanying text below tells us that the *gastaldo* (guild master) ordered the old sign from 1517 to be renewed. This yard built both galleys and merchant ships.

FV FATTO LANNO 1517 SOTTO MISIER ZACHARIA DANTONIO GASTALDO DE MARANGONI DNAVE D'LARSENAL FV RINOVATO D'LANNO 1753 SOTTO LA GASTALDIA DI FRANCESCO ZANOTTO GASTALDO E COMPAGNI

The managerial and administrative side made it necessary to build an office on the site.

In countries such as England and France the navy had a centralized organization. The English navy was run by a Board of Admiralty, the chairman of which – known as the First Lord – also sat in the government. The Board took the strategic decisions. In addition there was a Navy Board responsible for administration, management of the wharves and provisioning of the ships. At the head of each wharf there was a commissioner, usually an experienced naval officer.

Local organization

The way in which a navy was managed made very little difference to the way an arsenal was organized and designed. In principle the arsenal was responsible for the construction, maintenance and provisioning of warships. The general conditions an arsenal had to fulfil were: a large site on navigable water, gentle slopes, preferably close to a town that was a trading center. Space was important, since all the working areas, stores and warehouses had to be situated as ergonomically as possible. Naturally the warships themselves had to be able to sail out and dock there, but transport by water was equally necessary for the materials and other goods that had to be brought to the warehouses. The ships were launched from the gently sloping quayside; very few arsenals were equipped with a dry dock. Roofing over a slip was not usual, but in Venice some galleys were built under cover and by the end of the eighteenth century the same was true of some Swedish, English and French wharves. A nearby town was an advantage: the workers could then live in the vicinity. In addition the town would provide suppliers and merchants, able to furnish the materials and provisions required. The construction of

The National Sea Armory in Amsterdam, built in 1656, was the main arsenal of the admiralty of Amsterdam. This exceptional building has recently been restored; it has accommodated the Dutch Maritime Museum since 1973.

The impressive fleet at the disposal of Stadholder William III enabled him to ship a large army to England in 1688. This colored engraving by B. Stoopendaal shows the fleet lying off Hellevoetsluis, awaiting the sign to set sail. William III is taking his leave of members of members of the Dutch States-General, before embarking on his ship (at right) by means of a small riverboat.

In 1702 the combined English and Dutch fleets carried out an unsuccessful attack on Spanish squadrons at Cadiz with a view to obtaining a naval basis in the Mediterranean. On their way back, however, fortune did give the English-Dutch fleet the chance to capture a French squadron which accompanied a Spanish treasure fleet and was sailing out of the Bay of Vigo. They headed for home with rich rewards. Painting from c. 1705.

large wooden ships, whether these were the galleys of Venice or the later ships of the line, was incredibly labor intensive. Without exaggeration it can be said that in many nations the navy was the largest employer. Hundreds of carpenters could at any one time be seen crawling over the sloping sides of half-finished ships, porters and bearers were employed in the warehouses and at various other places all types of workmen could be found at their jobs. Except in Venice those employed in the naval wharves and arsenals usually did not enjoy military status. But the Venetian *Arsenalotti* were given military training which equipped them to carry out fire-fighting and policing tasks in the city. In addition to warehouses and shipbuilding installations some naval establishments had a number of buildings designed for unusual purposes. The arsenal of Venice, for instance, had a place where models and trophies were kept. In the Amsterdam admiralty's *Zeemagazijn* there was likewise a special area for

Between 1750 and 1850 a large number of coastal cities in Europe boasted a maritime arsenal.

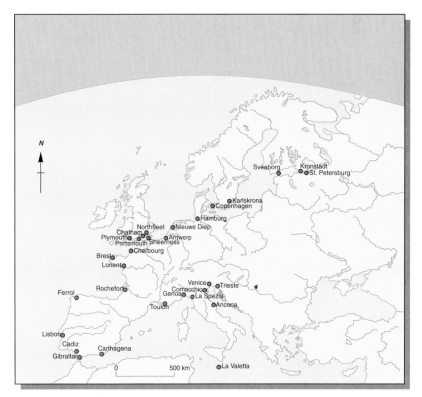

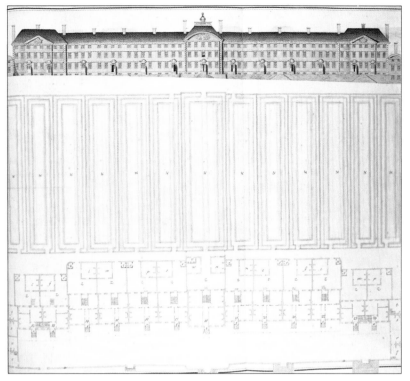

Sketch and groundplan of Officer's Terrace in the Plymouth Dockyard, c. 1690-1700.

models of ships. At the end of the eighteenth century in Karlskrona the famous architect Fredrik Chapman built a museum on the naval site to house his large collection of models. Some English and French arsenals even had a sizeable hospital. In Rochefort, for example, the hospital could accommodate four hundred patients. Even local townsfolk could avail themselves of the hospital's facilities. Smaller English wharves made use of de-commissioned ships as hospitals. These 'hulks' also acquired a sinister reputation when they were used as places of confinement for many thousands of prisoners of war, especially during the Napoleonic wars.

From drawing to ship

Before the eighteenth century a warship was not usually drawn before being constructed. The master shipbuilder generally had a scale model made which he then enlarged several times with his 'professional eye'. In some cases a 'plan' has been preserved, a detailed description of the ship under construction. Occasionally the planned shape of the vessel was 'drawn' on the slips as near to actual size as possible. Not much is known about the master shipbuilders. The time spent by the Russian czar Peter the Great in the Zaanstreek area and Amsterdam at the end of the

Cross-section of the *Hôtel de la Marine* at Versailles (c. 1750). Models of artillery pieces and strategic places, used for tactical plans, were kept on the lowest floor. The library with maps and floor plans was housed on the second floor, followed by two stories with meeting and study rooms. The top floor accommodated the printing presses; the floor below that the famous ship models that are now exhibited in the Navy Museum in Paris.

The arsenal at Graz

When the Turks conquered Constantinople in 1453, and in the following decade subdued the whole of the Balkan peninsula, two centuries of Ottoman threats to central European Christian culture and security ensued. After the battle of Mohàcs in 1526 the Ottoman Empire even laid claim to Hungary. As they bordered on the Holy Roman Empire, the central Austrian Habsburg duchies of Styria, Carinthia and Krain formed a line of defense for withstanding the Turkish forces, as well as a battleground for the first invasion (the *Sanntal*) in 1469. Many more invasions would follow, among them the famous campaigns by Sultan Suleyman in 1529 and 1532.

To counter these threats, the recruitment of soldiers for guarding the long borders was deemed necessary. The local populace also had to be armed to repel possible invasions. This required an adequate supply of all kinds of weapons and ammunition, produced from locally produced iron ore. The city of Graz, the capital of Styria and Austria's second largest city, became the central depository from where weapons were distributed to border strongholds to the south and east.

In the sixteenth century some of the arms supplies were kept in the attic of the *Landeshaus*, where the regional assembly met, whereas artillery was usually stored in local arsenals, the *Zeughütten*. This changed in 1642, when a huge arsenal was built next to the *Landeshaus*, the *Landeszeughaus*, designed by the Italian architect Antonio Solari. When building was completed in 1645, the main hall on the ground floor measured 50 x 7.40 m (162.5 x 24 ft) and contained all heavy artillery, while four stories of the same dimensions held the rest of the region's weapons and ammunition.

In 1700 the Ottoman menace had receded and the defense of the borders by local volunteers and mercenaries was taken over by a standing state army, armed by the Vienna War Council, the *Hofkriegsrat*. But in 1749 when the Austrian state wanted to take over the *Zeughaus* as well, to use the serviceable weapons and to sell off obsolete ones, the Styrian people asked Empress Maria Theresa to transfer the arsenal intact to the city of Graz, as a monument to bravery and duty in the struggle against the hereditary foe of Christianity. This request was honored by the Empress, and from that day to this the collection has remained unchanged. The collection comprises over 30,000 individual armaments, including over 3,300 suits of armor and helmets, 7,800 handheld firearms, as well as decorated weaponry for tournaments and the hunting excursions of the wealthy.

As the *Landeszeughaus* in Graz is now the world's only complete standing arsenal of its day it is a unique source for the study of armaments and a lasting monument of the Austrian popular defense against the Ottoman invaders.

This is part of a collection consisting of over 30,000 old weapons and coats of armor, still in the 16th century arsenal of Graz.

seventeenth century in order to acquire knowledge of shipbuilding is an exception to the normal pattern. During the first half of the eighteenth century the Amsterdam admiralty engaged the services of three Englishmen. Of one of these it is known that he had previously worked on the Danube and in Naples; another had acquired experience in Toulon. This bears witness to a certain degree of flexibility. The Swede Fredrik Chapman, son of an English immigrant, is also a prime example. In 1760 he returned to Sweden after years of working in wharves in England, France and Holland. The versatile nature of his work is to be seen not only in the shape of the models of the new ships which he designed but also in the buildings of the naval establishment in Karlskrona.

The timber needed for the ships was usually stored for years on site, generally in the water. In the Middle Ages Venice had been able to collect wood from its own hinterland. The Amsterdam admiralty had to look somewhat further afield: oak from southern Germany and other types of wood from countries along the Baltic. For the same reason English trading ships sailed to the north of Europe. The wharf's sawmill cut planks to size from the tree trunks. This was done using enormous saws in sawing pits or with the help of windmills. The task of bending outer planks into shape required the use of fire and water. The outer hull and the decks were fixed with wooden and iron fastenings. Iron was worked in the smithy. To seal the joints between the planks the workmen applied a mixture of shredded hemp and pitch, a task known as caulking. In order to protect the outer skin of the ship against the growth of marine organisms and the destructive work of the teredo worm, ships were fitted

in the eighteenth century with copper plates below the water line. Once the hull of the ship was ready it was launched. In Holland ships were built with their bows facing the water while in England it was the stern that faced out to sea. After launching, work progressed further on the water. The masts, often from the Norwegian forests, were fitted, with all the ropes and rigging. All cables and ropes were manufactured in the wharf's own rope walk, an extremely long building found on practically every wharf. Sail makers wove the especially heavy-duty sailcloth and sewed the sails to measure. Block makers turned out blocks in every shape and size. The interior of the ship was completely fitted out: bread holds, powder holds, special areas for storing cheese and other foodstuffs. A particularly remarkable phenomenon was the wood carving which graced these vessels. It was given a great deal of attention. The escutcheon, the flat stern, provided a particularly favorable area for the imagination of the wood carver and painter.

Fixed bunks in separate cabins in the stern of the ship were usually reserved for the captain and officers. The rest of the crew slept in hammocks slung from hooks fitted to the beams supporting the decks in the bows. Sometimes living and working accommodation was provided for the petty officers such as the gunner, responsible for weaponry, and the surgeon. The galley was the cook's territory, and he was helped by assistants. Because of the danger of fire the galley was always fitted with a stone floor, or even completely constructed in stone. Warships in particular, with their large cargo of gunpowder, were sensitive to open fires. Which is why the prescriptions covering the use of sources of light – candles and oil lamps – were particularly strict. Once the construction of the ship was completed, it had to be readied to sail and the stores delivered by the navy itself were loaded on board.

Stern of the Swedish royal battleship *Wasa*, which foundered on its maiden voyage in Stockholm harbor in 1628 due to a flagrant ballast mistake. The motifs and figures, completely covered in gold leaf, allude to the Bible and classical mythology. Reconstruction watercolor by Björn Landström.

In the 1960s the *Wasa* was salvaged and completely restored. The ship is on view in a roofed-over dry dock in Stockholm.

Admiral Cornelis Tromp's ship *De Gouden Leeuw*, the flagship of the Dutch fleet. Detail of the 'Battle of Kijkduin of August 21, 1673', painted by Willem van de Velde the Younger from a painter's ship. Like his father, van de Velde the Elder, he was commissioned with many a sea battle painting, either for the Dutch, or, should the occasion arise, for the English authorities.

Print on the frontispiece of *Aeloude en Hedendaegsche Scheeps-Bouw en Bestier* (Traditional and Contemporary Shipbuilding and Navigation) by Nicolaas Witsen, published in Amsterdam, 1671.

Furniture for the officers, the cook's kitchen equipment, the cannons, handguns, the sponges (for cleaning out the cannon barrels) and the gunpowder for the gunner, the nautical instruments and the charts for the helmsman – everything was carefully recorded and the users had to sign as proof of delivery.

Food and drink

In most European countries the navy was also responsible for the food and drink on board ships. Warships had fixed weekly menus, based on the most easily stored types of food. All the crew members of European warships ate hard bread and cheese and cooked meals of beans or peas with dried fish or salted meat. Drink was often ship's beer and small quantities of gin or brandy. Naturally water was carried, but this was mostly for cooking and could, in any case, only be kept for a limited period. The larger naval establish-

Armed soldiers embarking from Marseilles in 1753. Detail of the painting 'Harbor view' by Joseph Vernet painted in the same year.

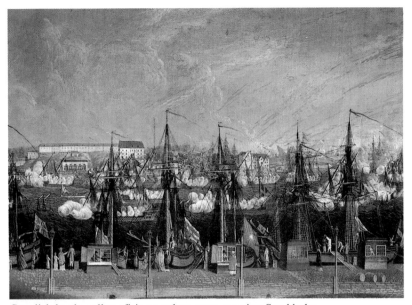

Swedish battle galleys firing a salute upon entering Stockholm harbor. During the 18th century Sweden and Russia were the only countries whose fleets still used galleys. The crew was not, however, made up of condemned criminals – as had previously been the rule – but of paid sailors and soldiers. Colored print from the 18th century.

In the course of the 18th century Russia built 400 galleys, which were to remain in service until 1806. Here the Swedish fleet and the Russian fleet of Czar Peter the Great joining battle at Hangö (1714). Engraving by Maurice Baquoy.

ments thus had their own abattoirs, bakeries and even breweries.

In Holland things were run differently, the admiralties delegating the responsibility for food and drink to the captains. At a fixed price per man per day it was the captain himself who saw to it that his vessel was provisioned.

Architecture

Most of the buildings on the site of a naval establishment had a purely functional character. An illustration depicting the Venice Arsenal, for instance, simply shows a number of wooden sheds. However in Amsterdam, and later in England, France and Sweden, in addition to functional buildings there was occasionally a structure with style. An example of one such is the *Zeemagazijn* of the Amsterdam admiralty. During the First English War of 1652 to 1654 the plans for a large naval complex picked up speed. The Amsterdam city architect Daniel Stalpaert was commissioned to design a central depot next to a new shipping wharf that was to be developed. His construction turned out to be an imposing square building, surrounded on three sides by water. Even at the time of its construction the *Zeemagazijn* was something of a tourist attraction and the poet Vondel wrote a great poem about it: the first completely classical warehouse in Holland. From 1658 the interested visitor was able to walk around inside the completed building. The various working areas and stores were grouped around a central inner courtyard. On the ground floor was the *herenkamer* (gentlemen's chamber) or, as it is nowadays known, the *Admiraliteitskamer* (the admiralty's chamber). There was also the model room, the equipment master's office and the storage space for nails and other metal objects. The first floor housed everything required for the rigging, plus such things as firefighting equipment. The second floor was the gunner's workplace, close to the weapons room with its many types of handguns. This floor also served as a storage place for the less expensive nautical instruments and the sails. In Plymouth a warehouse possibly modelled on the *Zeemagazijn* stood for close on a hundred years from the last decade of the seventeenth century.

The end

At the end of the eighteenth century it became clear that arsenals in their current form had seen their best days. At this period engineers all over Europe who were specialized in the building of harbors began to suggest a totally different approach to naval establishments. Apart from changing logistic demands, the rapid technological developments in shipbuilding materials and propulsion also brought about large-scale expansion. An overnight change of the infrastructure, based on wooden sailing vessels, to the construction of much larger iron and steel ships with complicated technology was obviously out of the question. Some arsenals could not be extended in any significant degree for lack of space or because the access route was not suitable for larger ships. However this did not mean immediate change, simply because of the enormous expenses involved. There is a story told about the costliness of the 'old' arsenals, related with reference to both El Ferrol and Karlskrona. In both cases, it would appear, the ruling monarch voiced doubts about the construction materials used: he remarked that there was no way they could be stone but must at least have been silver, as shown by the enormous costs. The materials used for the buildings where the successors to the wooden ships were to be constructed very likely were made of gold.

These British soldiers are clearly relieved at leaving their positions on the Western front during World War I.

The front soldier

Whatever the causes of a war, its theater of operations or the means
used to fight it, all were fought by soldiers who risked, and often lost, their
lives. They coped with privation as well as the danger of death;
and they were bound together by 'war's hard wire' – bonds forged by
comradeship, training, discipline and shared experience.

Richard Holmes

'War,' wrote Karl von Clausewitz, 'is nothing but the continuation of policy by other means'. In the Europe of the nineteenth and twentieth centuries such policy has had varied goals, among them self-defense, pre- serving the balance of power, national unification, re- straint of a threatening neighbor or naked territorial ambition. But whatever the causes of a war, its theater of operations or the means used to fight it, one central fact links battles as far apart in time and space as Albuhera (1811) and Arnhem (1944), Leipzig (1813) and Loos (1915), or Valmy (1792) and Verdun (1916). All were fought by soldiers who risked, and often lost, their lives; who coped with privation as well as the danger of death; and who were bound together by 'war's hard wire' – bonds forged by comradeship, training, discipline and shared experience.

Soldiers, by and large, are made, not born. Philos- ophers and psychologists squabble over whether or not man is inherently violent: a naked ape eager to revert to his primitive ways or a harmless herbivore corrupted by his environment. The American combat analyst S.L.A. Marshall – still a perceptive commen- tator even if his research methods would not meet today's criteria – observed that a recruit brought into the army the values of the society which produced him. In pre-1914 Europe an emphasis on manly vir- tues and the need to meet the coming challenge helped steel the generation that fought World War I to endure its miseries. One German soldier, describing the sen- sation of waiting to attack in March 1918, added: 'But at that time we were brought up though school and parental discipline in the spirit of the military Empire of the *Kaiser*'. A generation later, Henry Metelmann, a tank driver in the 24th Panzer Division, thought that while most of his comrades were not ardent Nazis, all

D. Raffet illustrated and idolized the bravery and dedication of Napoleon's *grognards*. Albeit with some occasional muttering, they would always follow their leader.

The twin heroes of the bloody Crimean War were the front soldier and the nurse. Many troops succumbed to cholera, as well as to war injuries. Florence Nightingale treated the troops both on the battlefield and in field hospitals.

In the Crimean War, Britain lost half its standing army. Many of the veterans were weakened by deprivation and illness.

were certain of the righteousness of their cause: 'I believed that it was my right to enforce our way onto others and for that reason I was doing a God-given job to go into other countries..'. Conversely, the future Marshal de Lattre de Tassigny blamed the French defeat of 1940 on the lack of 'moral order' in the Third Republic. 'The whole country has ceased to understand what effort means,' he wrote. 'This state of mind was indicated by the reduction of the working week and a constant preoccupation with leisure. Discipline disappeared. Leaders were criticized, discussed and disobeyed..'.

An army which recruited from a society emphasizing military values found that the schoolmaster had begun the drill sergeant's task. Louis Trochu, a French general of the Second Empire, thought that the Prussians had a great advantage. If you asked a Prussian soldier why he served in the army the man would reply: 'To serve my King and Country'. A French conscript would, however, respond: 'Because I drew a bad number [in the conscription lottery]'.

Whatever a recruit's background, the bonding process which began when he entered barracks was of fundamental importance in enabling him to do his job in the chaos of battlefield. The military oath, tracing its origins to the Roman *sacramentum*, was widely used in European armies. Often sworn on the regimental color in the presence of a man's comrades, the oath had a profound effect on many who took it. The American jurist Telford Taylor suggested that the fact that German soldiers swore a personal oath to Hitler between 1934 and 1945 was 'a seemingly insurmount-

The Crimean War saw the English, French and Austrian armies in an alliance with the Turks against the Russians. In 1855 the French Crimean War veterans paraded through the streets of Paris, celebrated as war heroes. Painting by E. Massé.

able obstacle to any decisive opposition to Hitler within the officers' corps'.

The uniform

The issue of a uniform accompanied the induction

Front soldiers in the firing line were the so-called 'cannon fodder'. Artillery fire killed or mutilated thousands of soldiers, before they even had a chance to offer any resistance. This picture shows victims of the battle of Solferino (June 24, 1859), which led to the foundation of the Red Cross.

At the outbreak of World War I, the soldier's standard equipment left much to be desired: it did not include a helmet or gas mask, and the battle dress was far too heavy.

process. Uniforms have both practical and symbolic functions. It keeps its wearer warm and dry, and – in the form of helmet, cuirass or flak jacket – may offer a measure of protection from sword, bullet or shell fragment. It also marks him out as a soldier among his fellow countrymen and distinguishes both his branch of service and his status within it. The practical has often been submerged by the symbolic, and on many battlefields men sweated under cumbersome headgear or struggled against constricting uniforms that looked elegant on parade but were less than ideal after a week's marching in the rain. In 1756 a soldier in the Prussian Regiment of Itzenplitz recorded that the combination of tight uniform with five different equipment straps passing across his chest was excruciating. 'The heat was so appalling,' he wrote, 'that I seemed to be walking on hot coals. I opened my shirt to let in a little air, and steam rose up as if from a boiling kettle'.

Uniforms became increasingly practical during the nineteenth century as weapon ranges increased, linear tactics were succeeded by more flexible groupings and concealment became desirable. First, rifle regiments, *Jäger* or *chasseurs* wore dull green rather than the bright scarlet or blue of their comrades of the line.

In 1917, during World War I, the area between Ypres and the North Sea, traditionally an affluent agricultural region, was turned into a wasteland. Without exception, the villages and cities of this area were reduced to flattened rubble in crater-riddled surroundings. This artillery column is passing through the devastated city of Ypres on September 27, 1917, en route to the front.

Later uniforms as a whole became less showy. The British army last wore its traditional red coats in battle in 1885, replacing them with khaki thereafter. The Prussians abandoned blue for *Feldgrau* on the eve of World War I, but French infantry retained long blue greatcoats and red pants until they were replaced by *bleu horizon* in 1915.

The arrival of somber-hued uniforms was not the end of the story. The thick serge of early twentieth century combat dress required frequent pressing to retain smartness in barracks, while on active service it was notoriously slow to dry. Only well on into the second half of the century did combat uniform became thoroughly practical. But an older symbolism remains. Many officers and NCOs wear badges of rank which their grandfathers would have recognized, and arm patches, qualification badges and colored berets mark a man's status and promote *esprit de corps*.

Automatic obedience

There was always more to pressing pants and polishing boots than mere cleanliness demanded. The recruit's specialization into the military has long involved basic training which emphasized unquestioning discipline, uniformity of appearance and the submersion of the individual within the group. For many years drill had an easily recognizable function: it helped soldiers move quickly and use their weapons efficiently at a time of acute personal crisis. Parade-ground drill survives as a shadow of the battle drill of the past. Its defenders argue that it still has its place, and the psychologist J.T. MacCurdy maintained that 'no one has as yet devised any other system which will so quickly inculcate the habit of automatic obedience'. There is a wider measure of agreement over the

After enduring the hardship and squalor of the trenches for months, the soldiers at the front found themselves defenseless against the added horror of gas attacks.

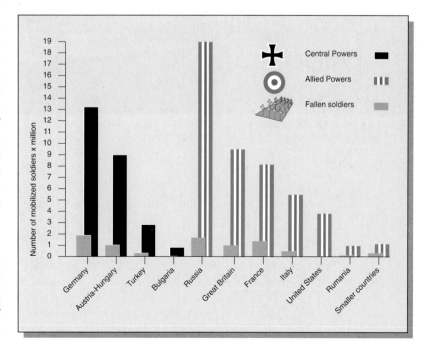

Number of soldiers mobilized and killed during World War I. Never before had the battlefields of Europe seen such huge armies joined in battle. Among the major belligerent nations the French and German armies had relatively the highest number of casualties.

The Great War is remembered as the most atrocious of all wars. This is an artist's impression of the ruins of Sas-Bos (province of western Flanders) in 1914, painted by M.H. Meunier.

Discharge of a British flame thrower, July 1, 1916. Flame projectors were installed in the front line, to cause confusion and affect the morale of the enemy.

need to train a soldier in drills which reflect the reality of battle. Essential tasks like changing a weapon's magazine or laying an artillery piece can be made almost instinctive by constant training, and tactical drills, which enable a unit to react promptly and without fuss to a given situation, are also of unquestionable value.

When the blank ammunition of maneuvers is replaced by the live rounds of battle the soldier reaps the bene-fit of all this preparation. Indeed, many analysts argue that a substantial proportion of combat effectiveness comes not from the more cerebral aspects of morale, but from solid training. The seasoned eighteenth century Russian campaigner Marshal A.V. Suvorov coined the maxim 'hard and heavy on the training ground, light on the battlefield,' and in his comparative study of German and U.S. combat performance in World War II, Martin van Creveld attributed a large measure of German success to superior training and organization.

The battlefield

Even the most realistic training rarely does full justice to reality, and a man's first experience of battle is often puzzling and disorientating. The battlefields of the horse and musket era were wreathed in the foul-smelling smoke of black powder. Stress narrowed the soldier's view of vision still further, so that he saw, not an artist's broad vista filled with neatly ranked figures, but a snapshot of his own small corner of the field. Yet the dense tactical formations of the past conferred psychological benefits on soldiers, and S.L.A. Marshall, writing of World War II, affirmed that: 'Man is a gregarious animal. He wants company. In his hour of greatest danger his herd instinct drives him

'The Harvest of Battle' is a cynical indictment against the barbarity of war. Despondency and numbness are evident on the faces of these soldiers returning from the front line. Painting by C. Nevinson.

towards his fellows. It is a source of comfort to him to be close to other men: it makes danger more endurable'. Sometimes peril induces a dream-like state. A World War I Australian infantryman wrote that 'I seemed to be in a sort of trance,' while a British soldier who fought at Ypres in 1917 described 'a peculiar, almost dream-like illusion'. Stress plays tricks on the memory. Time races or dawdles, specific events may slip beyond recall, blot out all else, or simply be put together in the wrong order, like strips of film reassembled haphazardly from the cutting-room floor. Before battle most soldiers are gripped by an apprehensive enthusiasm, eager to acquit themselves well but desperately anxious about what lies before them. Even before they glimpse the enemy they are assailed by terrible sounds. Shells rumble overhead or burst with a stunning crash nearby. Bill Mauldin, the American soldier-cartoonist who served in Europe during World War II, described how some shells sounded like 'rapidly ripped canvas,' while others had a 'two-toned whisper' or even a 'delicate shush-shush'. Rifle bullets crack overhead: an officer in the Spanish Foreign Legion described them arriving 'with all the hiss and spatter of a heavy storm'.

With all this comes recognition that death is in the air. Sometimes men are plucked from this world in an instant, hit by a bullet, blown to tatters by a shell or gulped lifeless by its blast. Often death comes more slowly, with spouting arteries or a sucking chest wound. The sight of the dead at first shocks soldiers, but many grow accustomed to the ghastly visions of the battlefield. Ernst Junger, a much-decorated World War I German infantry officer, wrote: 'Finally we were so accustomed to the horrible that if we came on a dead body anywhere on a fire-step or in a ditch we gave it no more than a passing thought and recognized it as we would a stone or a tree'. It is usually the wounded, rather than the dead, who dent all but the most robust professional detachment. An Australian who fought on the Somme in 1916 saw 'a man, not a bit of flesh not burnt, rolling around, waving his arm stump with nothing on it'. Raleigh Trevelyan could not even bring himself to describe fully the worst sight he saw at Anzio in 1944. 'There was something on a stretcher..'., he wrote, 'and it was still alive'.

Casualties

Over the past two centuries a wounded soldier's chance of survival has rocketed. Anesthetics ended the nightmare of surgery, whose agony might be dulled only by alcohol, opiates or partial strangulation. Joseph Lister's work on antisepsis led to the drastic reduction of post-operative infection: the

Passageways led from the trenches to the outposts and the land behind the river area. Convoys could only travel over them under the cover of the night, to supply and relieve the troops at the front at the end of their four-day shifts. Here an army doctor is examining the identity papers of a soldier killed in action (1914).

Edith Cavell, an English nurse, gave medical assistance to soldiers from all armies without distinction. During World War I, she treated prisoners of war, whom she had helped escape from German camps. She was executed by the Germans on October 12, 1915, after being taken prisoner during one such action. This painting by George W. Bellows from 1915 commemorates this brave nurse.

The international Red Cross

On June 24, 1859, there was a great battle near Solferino, a small place in Lombardy, between the Austrian and French armies. The battle was part of the Second Italian War of Independence and cost more than 29,000 lives. The Swiss banker, (Jean-) Henri Dunant (1828-1910), happened to witness the appalling conditions on the battlefield, where many wounded were simply left to fend for themselves. He decided to organize emergency relief for the victims of both sides.

Three years later he described his experiences at Solferino in *Un Souvenir de Solferino* and also suggested setting up a voluntary auxiliary service for the prevention and relief of suffering in war and peace, regardless of race or creed. Later, international agreements would also have to protect those wounded in war.

Dunant's ideas were given concrete form by four citizens of Geneva. With Dunant, they formed a Commission, and in 1863 they had a conference in which participants from 16 different countries took part and where the possibilities of implementing Dunant's ideas were discussed.

The following year the Swiss Federal Council organized a diplomatic International Convention. On August 22, 1864, in Geneva the first treaty was signed by 12 countries, who brought their national aid organizations together in the form of the International Red Cross (known in Muslim countries as the Red Crescent), and committed themselves to taking care of all those wounded in war. The highest consultative body was the Geneva Convention. Aside from this a maximum of 25 Swiss citizens formed an independent council (the International Commission), which in times of war functioned as an intermediary between the warring parties and the national Red Cross organizations.

This fast-acting, new humanitarian organization was quickly put to the test; in 1864 delegations were sent to the conflict between Denmark and Prussia, in 1870 an agency for help and information for the wounded and sick was opened in Basel, followed by similar organizations in Trieste (in 1877, during the Russo-Turkish War) and in Belgrade (during the Balkan Wars of 1912-13).

In the meantime Dunant had gone bankrupt and lived in poverty and oblivion, until he was 're-discovered' by a journalist in 1895. Finally, in 1901, he received honor and financial support, followed by the Nobel Peace Prize, which he shared with the pacifist Frédéric Passy, who had founded an international peace league in 1867.

Dunant's brainchild grew steadily and during World War I it focused particularly on improving the lot of prisoners of war. In the twentieth century the role of the Red Cross was extended, laid down during new Conventions, to encompass the protection of victims of war at sea (1907), prisoners of war (1929) and citizens in times of war (1949).

Peacetime activities included first aid, blood banks and care for the ill, handicapped, elderly, children and victims of national disasters. At the end of the twentieth century some of the tasks carried out by the Red Cross in times of war were taken over by UN peacekeepers.

A French Red Cross nurse at the front in 1914, painted by Romaine Brooks.

Anglo-Boer war of 1899-1902 was the first major conflict in which amputees were more likely to survive than to die of gangrene. Blood transfusions were used towards the end of World War I, and were routine in World War II. By that time penicillin and the sulphanomides helped reduce the danger of infection, and air transport speeded up the soldier's journey from battlefield to hospital. It was once axiomatic that illness killed more soldiers than bullets: in the Walcheren expedition of 1809 a British force lost 23,000 men to disease but only 217 to enemy action. Typhoid, cholera and an assortment of other ailments ravaged the armies of history, but the development of effective vaccines has greatly reduced their toll.

War breaks minds as well as bodies. Captain Cavalié Mercer, a British artillery officer at Waterloo, saw men who had fled 'not bodily to be sure, but spiritually, because their senses seemed to have left them'. During World War I it was often a matter of chance whether a victim of psychoneurotic breakdown was considered to be suffering from what British doctors termed 'shell shock' or was deemed a malingerer or a coward. National attitudes to psychiatric casualties have varied, making balanced comparisons difficult, but their sheer volume is striking. In March 1939, 120,000 former British servicemen were in receipt of pensions for primary psychiatric disability, and during World War II 1,393,000 American soldiers suffered psychiatric symptoms serious enough to debilitate them for some time.

War cemeteries, the last resting-place for hundreds of thousands of soldiers, are scattered throughout the area between the rivers Somme and IJzer. Every year, the Last Post is sounded in the memory of those who have died. These are the French war cemetery *La Maison Blanche* in Neuville Saint-Vaast (with wooden crosses), and the German cemetery of Menen.

Where World War I was a war of position, World War II was a *Blitzkrieg*, in which tanks played a large part. A German tank soldier surrendering (1942).

Soldiers have always died from accidents as well as hostile action. Clashes between friendly forces, the collapse of bunkers and dugouts and vehicle crashes, all imposed a steady drain of casualties. Men perished from exposure to the elements and long marches beneath a backbreaking load. Food, when it could be found, was often uninteresting, and shortages lowered men's defenses against cold or disease. Soldiers, particularly the poorly prepared Germans, suffered terribly on the Eastern Front in World War II. Sentries perished at their posts, weapons froze, sores and frostbite sapped morale. Even Western European winters are painful enough for men living in trenches or ruined buildings.

George Orwell wrote of his own experience of the Spanish Civil War that 'five things are important: firewood, food, tobacco, candles and the enemy. In winter on the Zaragoza front they were important in that order, with the enemy a bad last'.

Motivation

The majority of soldiers have managed to bear the twin burdens of enemy action and what Shakespeare termed 'rainy marching in a painful field'. They are sustained by a rich mixture of motives. Professional honor plays its part, especially for men brought up to value martial virtues. What an Australian termed 'the bonds of mateship' are also important: the resolve of many a soldier has been buttressed by his desire to show fortitude in the company of his comrades. Sometimes the death of a friend promotes a corrosive desire for revenge, and the grisly sequence of atrocity and counter-atrocity, so common in all too many wars, can sharpen the resolution of the combatants.

Most authorities agree that patriotism, useful though it may be to encourage men to enlist or to deter them from desertion, is of little use on the battlefield. However, ideological conditioning can help men cope with battle. Omer Bartov's study of German morale on the Eastern Front in 1941-1945 underlines the value of propaganda in fomenting hatred which nerved men to keep up the fight. It is also true that political divisions within a state may be reflected in its armed forces. Some Irish soldiers serving in the British army of World War I felt their loyalty strained after the Easter Rising of 1916, and in 1940 the cohesion of the Belgian garrison of Fort Eben Emael had been affected by friction between Flemish and Walloon soldiers.

A myriad of other motives keep men at the front. The sheer excitement of combat thrills some, while occasional flashes of natural beauty charm others. Drink or drugs may dull the hard edge of battle: the French divisions that took the Pratzen plateau at Austerlitz in 1805 had been liberally supplied with brandy, and a World War I British officer wrote that the air smelled of 'rum and blood' after an attack. Humor helps men cope, even if wartime jokes are often childish or

Invalids
of the Great
War were
filled with
indignation at
the poor
medical care
and ingratitude
which their
countries showed
towards them.
In 1928 Otto Dix
expressed
the contrast
between
the extravagance
of the roaring
twenties,
and the extreme
poverty of
a war invalid,
reduced to
beggary, on the
left panel of
his triptych
'Metropolis'.

This chart shows the combat efficiency of soldiers on the front, based on a study on the behavior of Allied soldiers after the landing in Normandy in 1944.

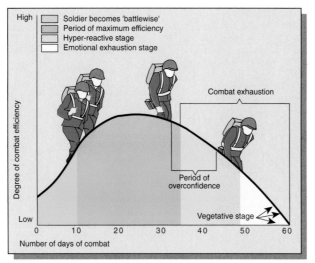

High

Soldier becomes 'battlewise'
Period of maximum efficiency
Hyper-reactive stage
Emotional exhaustion stage

Combat exhaustion

Degree of combat efficiency

Period of overconfidence

Vegetative stage

Low

0   10   20   30   40   50   60

Number of days of combat

macabre. Religion, too, plays its part in enabling soldiers to wait at death's door. Belief in the certainty of afterlife and a forgiving Savior comes easily to a man who may not see another dawn. Cynics jest about 'fire insurance', but there is much truth in the aphorism that 'there are no atheists in foxholes'.

Charismatic leadership also helps. In the Franco-Prussian War of 1870-71 a German explained that: 'When the lieutenant runs to the front, we must run with him'. In April 1809, as the French assault on Ratisbon wavered, Marshal Lannes grabbed a scaling ladder and began to drag it forward. His staff struggled to take it from him, and the sight inspired the nearby infantry, who rushed forward and took the town.

Leadership, comradeship, *esprit de corps* and a sense of duty all play their part in keeping men at the front. But they are rarely sufficient in themselves, and chains of discipline are needed to hold armies together. For much of history soldiers endured harsh corporal punishment: flogging was not abolished in the British army until 1881, and in most armies NCOs emphasized commands with a cuff on the head until very much later. For centuries too, the soldier who would not face the enemy's fire risked falling before that of his comrades. The death penalty was inflicted routinely in World War I – 346 British soldiers were executed, 266 for desertion – and in World War II both the Russian and the German armies reinforced discipline by liberal use of the firing squad and the commander's pistol.

For most Europeans the front soldier is rarely far away. The graveyards of the World Wars sprawl across the continent, with concentrations of suffering marked by memorials like the Douaumont ossuary at Verdun, which shrouds the bones of perhaps 170,000 men. Smaller monuments mark many earlier conflicts. A pillar on the 1757 battlefield of Kolin pays tribute to the Walloon Dragoons, and the losses suffered by the Prussian Guard on August 18, 1870, are remembered by memorials lining the St. Privat crest outside Metz.

Veterans dwindle as the years go by, but gray-haired figures with medals shining on their chests still gather to remember fallen comrades, and ex-servicemen's organizations remind governments that men who risked their lives, health and sanity in their youth deserve continuing care as age and infirmity add their weight to the strains imposed by war. As the twentieth century nears its close, it is tempting to hope that the experiences of the front soldier will become a matter of historical reflection. But the pattern of history gives us little cause for confidence, and Europe will be fortunate indeed if she does not continue to ask her young men to visit the cruel old world of war.

German troops on the Russian front during a winter day in 1942.

An overcrowded British army field hospital on the day following D day. Detail of the 'Overlord' tapestry, which was made in memory of this event.

Mass armies and industrial warfare

War in the nineteenth and twentieth centuries

Mankind adapted the inventions and results of the Industrial Revolution to give warfare another dimension. The Industrial Revolution was also closely related to the nation states in which it was able to come to fruition. The combination of the Industrial Revolution and nationalism allowed larger armies to be brought into the field. These mass armies were to thoroughly influence the face of war in the nineteenth and twentieth centuries.

Luc de Vos

'War', painted by Otto Dix in 1914, is an evocation of the destruction caused by modern warfare, with its modern technology and scenes of chaos. The lines crisscrossing the canvas represent the destructive power of artillery fire.

From 1771 to 1774 father and son Verbruggen from The Hague (the Netherlands) modernized the gun foundry of the English Woolwich Brass Foundry. They precisely recorded the whole gun-founding process in aquarel drawings like this one.

The Industrial Revolution and the mass armies

The Industrial Revolution first saw the light of day in Great Britain. This meant that the British were the first to be able to produce firearms in large numbers in a short period of time. Between 1793 and 1815 they produced approximately three million of the 'Long-land Pattern India'. This firearm was less accurate than the French one, having neither a sight nor a bead. The large space between the projectile and the barrel also contributed to the weapon's inaccuracy.

The Prussian general Carl von Clausewitz set down the ideas about war of his day. In his eyes the ultimate aim of war was the total defeat of the enemy. When anything at all was conceded to the loser it was a *Halbding*. Clausewitz' ideas attracted a great deal of attention in Germany and spread from there throughout the Western world. They have set the tone in military thinking up till the present day.

The Friedrich Krupp AG cast steel factory in Essen was the main weaponry-producing factory in Germany during World War I. One third of the guns and one tenth of all ammunition for the German army was produced here. During the war years the production was constantly stepped up.

Around 1850 there was an important breakthrough in weapon technology. Rifled barrels replaced smooth barrels very rapidly. Furthermore, the weapons were no longer loaded through the barrel but through the breech. The result was that the accuracy and firing

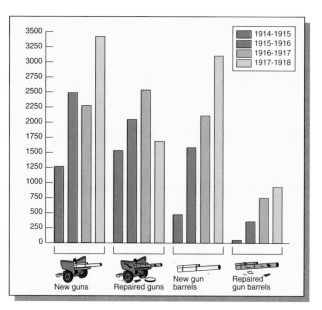

rate of the weapons increased greatly. These weapons caused a real slaughter amongst the too compact armies on the battlefields of Magenta and Solferino. This was the context in which the Swiss Henri Dunant set up the Red Cross in 1859 with the aim of helping the many wounded in military conflicts.

The technological breakthrough in the year 1850 was not decisive in the Franco-Prussian War of 1870-1871. Although the Germans had better cannons, the French chassepot rifle was superior. The German success can be attributed more than anything to other factors. As a result of lot drawing and substitution systems the French army had stayed relatively small. The armies of Prussia and the other German states were, because of generalized conscription and the demographic explosion, significantly larger. Furthermore, the academically formed German officers succeeded in concentrating the numerous troops in the right places at the right times through using the strategically laid out railway lines. In this way a united German army could do battle with a disunited French army. The French defeat seemed total. The French people, however, managed to prolong the struggle through guerilla warfare. The uprising of the Parisians against the traditional authorities heralded in a new chapter. The establishment chose to suppress the Commune and temporarily accept the predominance of the now united Germany.

The First World War, mass armies and mass production

At the end of the nineteenth century the most populous state in West and Central Europe, Germany, was also the most industrialized. In industrial development

Belgian riflemen on their way to the front; their machine guns are drawn by dogs (c. 1914).

In 1851 Alfred Krupp set about manufacturing small guns in his father's steel mill. He used the profits of this venture to set up a new factory for the manufacture of larger guns and ammunition. After the development of the Siemens-Martin furnace, the effective range of these guns was substantially improved, resulting in a large number of orders from countries around the world. The Krupp factory in 1875, bustling with activity, painted by Adolph Menzel.

British soldiers abandoning their positions en masse under the threat of a gas attack. Painting by John Nash.

it was closely followed by Great Britain, Belgium and France. The process of industrialization was also underway in parts of Russia, Austria (now the Czech Republic) and in North Italy. There was great rivalry for raw materials and markets. Africa and Asia were nearly completely colonized by this stage. The generalized provision of elementary education was one of the foundations for the spread of a cliched vision of neighboring countries. France dreamed of revenge. It wanted to reconquer the border provinces it lost in 1871, Alsace and Lorraine. This tension between the Germanic and Latin worlds had a counterpart in the Balkans. Serbia dreamed of snatching the mosaic of nations, Bosnia and Herzogovina, from the multi-

In 1915 chemical weapons were used for the first time in the history of warfare. The poisonous gas *yperite* derived its name from the area near Ypres, where many soldiers fell victim to its lethal effects.

national Austria-Hungary. Here the German world was confronted with the Slavic. The powder keg exploded in the Balkans. Europe fell prey to an inflated nationalism. The fear of being in the minority led to a rapid mobilization. Germany took the side of Austria-Hungary and attacked France. It hoped to defeat its large western neighbor before Russia was ready to enter the arena. Russia itself thought it could rise above its internal problems by presenting itself as the champion of the Slavic and Orthodox peoples. The preceding block formation led to a chain reaction amongst the armies drawing out onto the battlefield.

Those things that were invented at the end of the nineteenth century were now put into action: submarines, reinforced concrete, artillery with a cradle and brake system and goniometer and, above all, machine guns. The acme of the time's industrial capacity, the battleship, hardly left the harbor. The mighty British fleet was able to, through its presence, keep the German fleet in port. The British used their fleet according to the formula of the American admiral Alfred Thayer Mahan as a "fleet in being".

The German mass army of 3,800,000 men, 6% of the German population, seemed at first to be going to surpass the successes of 1870. The equally numerous French army, made up of 9% of the French population, managed, however, to bring the enemy to a halt with British and Belgian help. In November 1914 the

In 1929, on the eve of the Great Depression, René Magritte painted 'On the threshold of freedom', a premonition of another destructive war.

Well-equipped soldiers of the large German army listening to the speech of their charismatic leader, Hitler, at the mass meeting of Nuremberg in 1933.

109

In 1940, French troops only travelled on foot or on horseback, which put them at a serious disadvantage with the motorized German army. The famous 75-mm gun used by the French army was an excellent artillery piece, but no match for the German tanks. With hindsight, one can say that the French generals, although well versed in the tactics of World War I, had no eye for the requirements of modern warfare.

A British tank attack in the Western Desert

BACK THEM UP!

front was fixed from the North Sea to Switzerland. The two sides dug themselves in. Only trenches offered protection from the merciless fire from rifles, machine guns and cannons. Both sides seemed to be checkmated.

The fundamental military problem in World War I was that of making a breakthrough. Bombardment from a distance, the use of gas, flamethrowers and loads of dynamite that were exploded under the enemy's lines all brought no solution. Mass attacks led to genuine slaughters. Towards the end of the war the armored tank moving on tracks seemed to offer a solution. It was, however, the 1.8 million American soldiers who, in 1918, finally tipped the balance. A non-European state settled the dispute on the old continent. For the time being, however, France and Great Britain continued to have the leading word. In the meantime a change of regime had been brought about in the largest of the peripheral states, Russia. A civil war had given the power to the revolutionary Communists.

In the eyes of many World War I was a return to the barbaric wars of the mass migrations of the early Middle Ages. In the mass armies men were reduced to a piece of easily replaceable material. The British general and historian Fuller asserted that a human life was as cheap as dirt. The process of democratization had brought the war so close to the whole population that a war was felt as a matter of 'Sein oder Nichtsein'. Between 1914 and 1915, 600,000 men volunteered to

The deployment of tanks in massive numbers enabled the Germans to achieve major successes over their opponents in the early stages of World War II. This British poster, printed in 1942-1943, was intended to ward off the fear of the advancing panzers.

join the British army. But it was still necessary in 1915 for the United Kingdom to introduce general conscription to be able to keep on feeding the God of War.

The radicalization of World War I was not just a result of general conscription and the involvement of the whole population but also of the thoroughgoing industrialization of the war. In 1815 at Waterloo, Napoleon had the use of approximately 20,000 artillery projectiles which weighed about 100 tons altogether. For the battle of the Somme in June 1916, the British had amassed 3 million shells weighing approximately 20,000 tons. In 1917, during the battle of Malmaison, the French fired off 80,000 tons of ammunition in six days, about 10 million shells. To transport that amount they needed 226 trains of 30 wagons each. One month

Workers on an assembly line of artillery shells in a French ammunition factory which employed many women during the war.

was necessary for the preparations. The battles of Verdun and Ypres, between the French and the Germans and the British and the Germans respectively, displayed the war in all its gruesomeness. The modern technology wreaked havoc. In the few dozen square miles around Ypres approximately 200,000 British soldiers were killed; and still the front did not move. Today the 142 British military cemeteries around Ypres still form a silent witness to so much human suffering.

Europe emerged from World War I greatly weakened. Belgium alone had lost approximately 18% of its national wealth as expressed in machines, buildings, bridges, fields and money. Germany too had paid a high price. It had called 13 million to arms. At the end of the war military service was required from age 17

This pacifist poster for the Belgian Socialist Party (1930) portrays the British prime minister attempting to call off the arms race of 1914-1924 set in motion by the French and Italian governments.

up to 60! Germany had 1.9 million soldiers to mourn. France, with a significantly smaller population, had lost 1.3 million men from the 8.2 million called up. The regional recruiting and the large numbers of dead resulted in the depopulation of particular areas and had dramatic results. Europe had mobilized almost 70 million soldiers of whom about 8 million ended up losing their lives.

The Allies' final victory was largely due to the U.S. intervention in the war. At the peace negotiations in Versailles and other places near Paris the American president Woodrow Wilson achieved little more than the foundation of the League of Nations and the break-up of Austria-Hungary. His own country drew itself back into isolationism and left quarrelsome Europe to its fate. The British prime minister Lloyd George and his French counterpart Georges Clemenceau helped themselves.

In the early 1930s Europe came into difficulties itself, partially because of the depression in the U.S. These economic difficulties and the German dissatisfaction about its territorial, military and economic limitations helped Adolf Hitler's totalitarian and populist regime to power. Hitler enthused and re-armed his country. After indulgence on the part of the Western democracies had lead to the absorption of Austria, the Sudetenland and Bohemia-Moravia, World War II broke out in September 1939. Poland was wiped off the map. Hitler had first covered himself in the East by means of a giant's alliance with the other totalitarian state, the Soviet Union.

World War II, mass armies and elite troops

On May 10, 1940, all hell broke loose in the west. At that moment Germany had 6 million soldiers, 6% of its population, under arms. The breakthrough in the Ardennes, the crossing of the Meuse and the astonish-

Title page of the German magazine *Illustrirte Zeitung*, 1917. In the same year a campaign was started to raise financial support for the construction of U-boats, the German submarines. From the initial stages of World War II these U-boats proved a very active and dangerous threat to the British merchant fleet. Submerged, the speed of these vessels did not exceed three to four knots, but on the surface they could easily reach ten knots, which is quite fast. During the war, the Germans developed no less than twenty types of U-boats.

The German navy organized fleet shows at regular intervals, to brush up its image among the public at large. Here the German fleet is sailing from port, a huge imperial eagle at the stern of every ship. Watercolor by Willy Ströwer.

Anti-missile demonstrations in Europe

At the time of the Cold War, Europe was divided into East and West. In terms of political relationships that meant the Warsaw Pact and NATO countries. For decades both sides concentrated on building up their arsenals of, in particular, nuclear weapons. In 1969 talks began between the two superpowers (the USA and the USSR) with the goal of slowing down the arms race. The first SALT Treaty (Strategic Arms Limitation Talks) was signed in 1972 and set maximums for the numbers of intercontinental missiles and nuclear submarines.

Towards the end of the 1970s, the Soviet Union decided to replace its obsolete SS-4 and SS-5 missiles with the new SS-20, with a range of 3,000 miles. This was viewed by Western leaders as an attempt to bring Western Europe into the Soviet sphere of influence. The reaction to this new balance of power, in which NATO was clearly at a disadvantage (for the middle range, NATO had only fighter planes equipped with missiles), was the dual decision of December 12, 1979: 464 Tomahawk cruise missiles and 108 Pershing II missiles would be stationed in European NATO member countries starting at the end of 1983, if in the meantime negotiations with the East Bloc had not led to a reduction. Two weeks later, the Soviet Union invaded Afghanistan, and the new long-range treaty (SALT II) was not ratified by Congress.

The planned stationing of 572 American middle-range nuclear warheads heightened the possibility of a nuclear war between the superpowers fought on European soil. The result was broad and intense public protest. On October 10, 1981, 300,000 people gathered to demonstrate in Bonn. On November 21, 1981 400,000 Dutch demonstrated in Amsterdam against nuclear armament. In that same year, the INF (Intermediate-range Nuclear Forces) talks on middle-range weapons began in Geneva. A year later, the actual reduction of strategic nuclear weapons became the subject of negotiations (START: Strategic Arms Reduction Talks).

In 1983, these talks had still not produced any results. The European peace movement was at its zenith that year. On January 21, 1983, the British newspaper *The Guardian* held a national survey: it appeared that 61 percent of the British were against the proposed stationing. A clear majority was against the new missiles in West Germany, the Netherlands, Belgium and Italy as well.

The women's peace camp at the U.S. military base Greenham Common in England, as well as the hunger strike by demonstrators at the missile base Comiso in Sicily, attracted worldwide attention. All sorts of small organizations, including many religious groups, united in a common goal. Massive demonstrations were the result: on October 29, 1983, the Dutch seat of government, The Hague, was flooded with more than a half million protestors and more than 1.2 million people took part in the German activity week in October 1983. On October 22, as part of these activities, 150,000 demonstrators joined hands, creating a human chain 67 miles long between Stuttgart and Neu-Ulm. Despite the widespread unease, the governments of the European NATO members decided to allow placement of the missiles.

Fortunately, the arrival of Gorbachev meant conciliation at the negotiating table: the INF treaty was signed on December 8, 1987. This treaty called for the destruction of all land-based middle-range nuclear warheads on both sides within three years. It was a major step on the way to the end of the Cold War.

During the 1980s hundreds of thousands of demonstrators marched against the deployment of nuclear missiles in their countries in various European capital cities.

ing advance on the mouth of the Somme, however, were all the work of a small elite. At the most, 300,000 men were able to make the breakthrough and exploit it by using tanks and airplanes in combination. After a few days the campaign in the west was virtually won. What followed was the collapse. Professional soldiers, nonconformist tactical thinking and a limited quantity of modern weapons dealt the mass armies a heavy blow. The German Third Reich seemed to be the great victor. Western continental Europe was united under its rule. Only Great Britain stubbornly struggled on. Germany's attack on the Soviet Union in June 1941, however, offered new perspectives. When Japan attacked the U.S. at the end of the year the European war became a genuine World War.

The U.S., which had a smaller army than Denmark in 1939, was able to set up a gigantic war machine in a very short time due to its industrial potential. In the course of the war it produced 300,000 airplanes,

In 1940, the British Royal Navy had six aircraft carriers in its service, only one of which complied with the standards of the day. The ship-bomber combination proved extremely successful during the attack on the Italian fleet in the port of Taranto.

During the battle of England the British pilots used a radar system which was much more advanced than its German counterpart. The ground control system, which directed the aircrafts from second to second and only launched them into battle at the most opportune moment, was of decisive importance.

86,000 tanks and more than 1,000 warships, including 27 large and 110 small aircraft carriers. Great Britain, too, produced an enormous effort and built 128,000 airplanes and 7 large and 45 small aircraft carriers. The industrial feats of the Soviet Union are often ignored. It is all too often thought that that country only supplied cannon fodder. In 1944 it produced 30,000 tanks and 48,000 airplanes. Germany defended itself against so much industrial violence. It produced more than 100,000 airplanes. It attempted to use the retaliatory weapons V1: the unmanned dynamite loaded aircraft, V2: the ballistic rocket, V3: the super-cannon, and the Messerschmidt 262 jet to defend fortress Europe. Shortages of raw materials and in particular of petroleum and the 2 million tons of bombs dropped on Europe by the British and the American air forces made the struggle very unequal.

In May 1945 the Thousand-Year Reich no longer existed. Now that the stipulation "Europe first" had been satisfied, Japan could be finished off as well. The atomic bombs on Hiroshima and Nagasaki in August 1945 broke Japan's last resistance. Had the era of scientific warfare dawned?

Europe emerged from World War II even more weakened than from WWI. The Soviet Union lost approximately 17 million inhabitants, Germany 5 million, Poland 4.5 million. Both France and Great Britain lost half a million more than the U.S., which had 300,000 soldiers to mourn. Even Belgium lost more people,

Stukas *(Sturzkampfflugzeuge)* were bombers flying in formation the greater part of their flight, but each attacking in an individual nosedive. These aircraft had a two-person crew, three machine guns and could carry up to 500 kg (1100 lbs) of bombs. In 1940, the allied bombers were inferior to the German ones, due to a lack of numbers and quality.

approximately 50,000, than Canada, approximately 40,000. The Netherlands lost about 200,000 people of whom half were Jewish. The drama of the Jews in Europe would lay the foundation for the resurrection of the Jewish state in the Middle East in the historic land of Palestine. Expressed in economic terms World War II cost five times as much as WWI. The U.S. was henceforth fabulously wealthy: 80% of all the world's gold lay in Fort Knox.

At the great conferences of 1945, Yalta and Potsdam, it was chiefly the U.S. and the Soviet Union who determined the fate of Europe. The United Kingdom was tolerated but Western and Central Europe had absolutely no right to speak. Nevertheless it was in Europe that the Cold War began shortly thereafter. Europe was divided into the spheres of influence of the two superpowers, the U.S. and the Soviet Union. Germany was transformed into a giant barracks and an unprecedented arms race was begun.

Scientific warfare and the path back to professional armies

The nationalization of the Suez Canal led, in 1956, to British and French intervention. Under the combined pressure of the two superpowers, however, the two European states were forced to make a humiliating withdrawal. The conclusion of the United Kingdom

The British Spitfire was a combat aircraft intended to recapture the initiative in the air from the Stukas, which were defenseless when operating individually. The Spitfire was a maneuverable one-man aircraft, which could rise to an altitude of 3,500 m (11.375 ft) in 4 min 8 sec, and carried 8 machine guns. It was lighter than the heavy, slow Stukas, and consequently effective in pursuit and quick to take aim.

was that from then on nothing was possible without the support of the great Anglo-Saxon brother, the U.S. France, on the other hand, persisted in its belief that a united Europe offered the only solution. It built its own atomic weapons, the 'Force de Frappe', and by means of the European Economic Community prepared, with Germany, for the autonomy of the Occident.

In the meantime Europe's humiliation continued. The decolonization in the late '50s and '60s seemed the absolute end. In reality it was a new beginning. Freed from the colonial burden and protected by the American atomic umbrella, Europe worked on an unprecedented economic flowering. The U.S. soon found itself in great difficulties because of its involvement in the Vietnam drama. In the early '80s the Soviets became entangled in the war in Afghanistan.

Armed concrete shelters, called bunkers, were equipped with anti-aircraft artillery as part of the *Atlantikwall* which stretched along the Dutch, Belgian and northern French North Sea coastline, as far south as the Gironde estuary near Bordeaux.

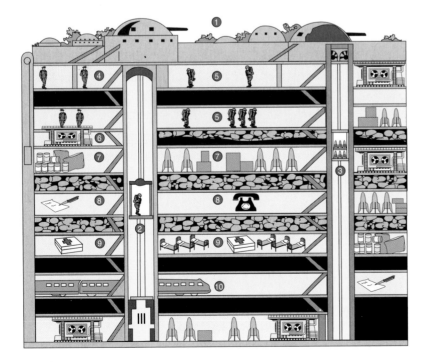

The arms race continued until the Soviet Union, bled to death, threw in the towel. This first became apparent in 1985 and was definitive by 1989. Germany was reunited and Europe became a continent once more. In 1991 the U.S. showed what it was capable of militarily. Its professional, electronically equipped army gave an unprecedented display in the Gulf War. It was militarily and politically the only superpower but in a bad situation economically.

Meanwhile Europe found itself confronted with ethnic, religious and bluntly nationalistic problems in the Balkans. There seemed no military answer to these new sources of conflict. Professional military units from Western and Eastern Europe attempted "peace-keeping" activities. All of Western Europe is being confronted by the disappearance of the possibility of a large conventional conflict and the appearance of numerous small conflict areas with the question as to whether or not the conscript armies should be replaced with professional ones.

A publication in Stalin's name once classified war as being artisanal, manufacturing and industrial. In the last phase the size of the armies seemed to continuously increase. Whereas Napoleon brought 70,000 men to the battlefield at Waterloo, World War II saw armies of millions opposing each other. The dimensions of the slaughter have more or less followed the same pattern. Today's technological and sociological evolution has lead to a decline in the size of armies. Could this be an important feature of a new phase, the scientific?

The superiority in this area of the U.S. and of a Western Europe that lives in a technological culture is still apparent. But what will happen in a very rapidly developing Southeast Asia?

Today there are three sorts of possible conflicts: nuclear, classical and revolutionary. In the first kind of conflict science is dominant, the second is becoming more and more a combination of the industrial and the scientific and the third is based most of all on human emotions.

Although the U.S. is superior in the area of nuclear weapons the nuclear arsenals of France, Great Britain and the Ukraine are not to be discounted. Russia too, a half European and half Asiatic land, still has megatons of destructive potential at its disposal. Today, the concern in that land is rising as regards the administration and protection of this arsenal – not to mention the prevention of the emigration of nuclear scientists to Third World countries anxious to develop their own nuclear weapons.

Cross-section of a bunker of the Maginot line, the impressive line of defense built on the eastern borders of France during the years after World War I. These costly defense works have never been tried, since the Germans attacked France via Belgium.
1. Bunkers with gun turrets; 2. Passenger lift; 3. Goods lift; 4. Officers' quarters; 5. Soldiers' quarters; 6. Diesel engines for ventilation and electricity generation; 7. Administration and telephone exchange; 8. Food and ammunition supplies; 9. Medical supplies and hospital; 10. Train link.

Picasso painted his anti-Fascist work 'Guernica' for the Spanish pavilion at the World Exhibition of 1937 in Paris. He refused to let the work be brought to Spain as long as his country was not a true democracy, in spite of the fact that the Spanish government had officially bought the work. The painting was not exhibited in Madrid until 1981. This detail is an evocation of the destruction and the human suffering which the heavy German bombardment of the small town of Guernica brought about.

The enemy within

The Spanish civil war

From July 18, 1936, until April 1, 1939, Spain was embroiled in a long and bitter Civil War which, because of its violence and its ideological and political connotations, stirred the conscience of the Western world. Both seen as a crusade against Communism and idealized as the romantic resistance of the people and the proletariat against Fascism, the Spanish Civil War is perhaps best described as a 'fantasy of the people' in which heroism and atrocities, intolerance and fanaticism, hate and fear coexisted.

Juan Pablo Fusi Aizpúrua

On April 14, 1931, Spain became a republic after a peaceful transfer of power, an event which the old Republicans and the intellectuals regarded as evidence of the political maturity of the country.

The coalition government and the separate regions of the young Spanish Republic were deeply divided over the reform program which the government wanted to implement. These divisions led to chaotic situations and revolt. Here rebellious miners are arrested in Asturia (1932-1933).

On July 18, 1936, part of the Spanish army rose against the Republican Government, the democratic regime set up in 1931 in accordance with the will of the people. From then until April 1, 1939, Spain was embroiled in a long and bitter Civil War which, because of its violence and its ideological and political connotations, stirred the conscience of the Western world. The Right saw the Civil War as a crusade against Communism; the Left idealized it as the romantic resistance of the people and the proletariat against Fascism. Manuel Azaña (1880-1940), the Republican leader, Head of the Government from 1931 to 1933 and President of the Republic from the spring of 1936, an intellectual distressed by the tragedy of his country, saw it differently – as a 'fantasy of the people' in which heroism and atrocities, intolerance and fanaticism, hate and fear coexisted.

The Spanish Civil War became international in nature. The Fascist powers, Germany and Italy, openly assisted the military uprising with arms and men. The USSR aided the Republic and the International Brigades, a large contingent of volunteers mostly supporting Communist ideology, fought on its side. The Civil War was however Spanish. Azaña pointed out that the War originated as a result of the discord within the middle classes and the Spanish bourgeoisie in general – who were deeply divided for religious and social reasons.

He was right. The fall of the monarchy and the proclamation of the Republic in April 1931 were not only a change of regime. With the Republic came great hope of social change. The Socialist/Republican Coalition, which governed the country from 1931 to 1933 under Azaña, started an ambitious program of reforms of what it considered were Spain's major problems. It wanted to dispossess the large landowners and distribute the land among the peasants and to create a new Army which first and foremost was to be professional and apolitical. The Coalition sought to limit the influence of the Catholic Church, to secularize social life and promote liberal, secular education and, finally, to remove the State's overall authority giving independence to the regions with different languages and cultures – Catalonia, the Basque Country and Galicia – where there had been strong nationalist movements since the end of the nineteenth century.

The Government's plans polarized political and social life. Reforms led to opposition and to rejection of the Catholic viewpoint, of the Church, landowners and many of the armed forces. Some of the Government initiatives, such as land reform, were poorly conceived. In other cases, such as suppression of the Jesuits or prohibition of religious orders teaching, the Government acted with excessive and unnecessary sectarianism. Consequently, it alienated the support of important groups of the urban and rural middle classes. On the other hand, its measures were insufficient to satisfy large sectors of the working classes and country people. Some did not give the Government time; the anarchist Syndicalist trade unions of the General Workers' Union (CNT) launched a revolutionary offensive against the Government as early as the summer of 1931.

The military uprising

As a result, the political movement towards democratic stability was soon in trouble. The elections of 1933 marked a significant turn towards the Right. A Cath-

Salvador Dali created his hallucinatory study 'The foreshadowing of war' in 1934. It expresses his fear of the imminent civil war, which many Spaniards felt in their bones.

A water carrier on a square in Toledo. Note the multitude of posters calling on the people to support the Popular Front (1936).

The Falangist death squads, belonging to the Spanish Fascist party, the *Falange*, advancing on Seville by way of Cantillana (1936). Political murders and reprisals were commonplace events at the time.

in a Popular Front headed by Azaña, won the election again in February 1936, on July 18, 1936, a group of Right wing army officers staged the Coup. Some officers had however rebelled in North Africa the previous day.

Only part of the Army rebelled. The troops, led by generals Franco, Sanjurjo, Mola and Queipo de Llano, came out for several reasons: they believed that the Republic was a regime with no political authority; that granting independence to the regions threatened the unity of Spain; that the strikes and disorders showed that the democracy lacked authority; that the legislation of the Republic attacked the very essence of

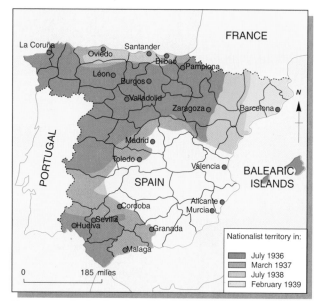

Four stages in the development of the Spanish Civil War. Slow but sure, the Nationalists conquered the whole country of Spain.

olic party which had broken away from the idea of a Republic, the Spanish Confederation of Independent Right Wingers (CEDA), became the key to power in 1934 and 1935, 'two black years' during which a large proportion of the legislation passed between 1931 and 1933 was amended to suit Conservative views. The Socialist party, the principal force of the Left, fearing Spanish Fascism, chose to rebel. The unsuccessful Socialist Revolution of October 1934, which led to hundreds of deaths and left many thousands of people in prison, seriously harmed the authority of the Republican regime. As a result, when the Left, united

On July 8, 1936 General Franco, in Morocco at the time, called a revolt against the Republic. He had a huge fresco painted, portraying himself as a true crusader accompanied by the national knight-apostle St. James of Santiago, who once upon a time led the Spanish to victory over the Muslims.

Catholicism in Spain. The rebel forces believed that the Coup would succeed immediately. They were wrong. They had started a devastating Civil War which lasted for three years.

The military uprising only succeeded in part of Spain – in Galicia, Navarre, Alava, Old Castille, the capital of Aragon, some cities in Andalusia, the Canary Isles and the Balearics (except Minorca) and in the North African colonies. It failed in Madrid, Catalonia, the Levant, the provinces along the north coast, in the center south of Spain, a large part of Andalusia and in Aragon. Out of the 31,000 officers of the Spanish army in 1936, about 14,000 rebelled; about 8,500 remained loyal to the Government; the remainder suffered different fates. The Republic had about 160,000 troops, and a large proportion of the Air Force and the Navy. The rebels, who called themselves 'Nationals', retained about 150,000 troops, among which were the elite of the Army, the Moroccan Army of about 47,000 men which Franco very quickly airlifted to Spain with German and Italian help.

Although the two sides appeared equal in strength, one essential point was not apparent – owing to the very nature of the people's response to the Coup, there was no united political and military leadership of the war on the Republican side for several months. The

Families on the run along the coast of Malaga, their scant belongings packed on mules.

military rising unleashed a revolution of the working class which, under the leadership of the Workers' Party and Trade Unions, broke the structure of the Republican State. It was this which led the Spanish Civil War to stir the imagination of the European Left,

Socialists and Communists from many countries went to Spain in order to enforce the Republican Army. They are commonly referred to as 'International Brigades'. Estimates of their number vary largely. Apart from combatants, some 10,000 doctors, nurses and technicians had volunteered for the International Brigades.

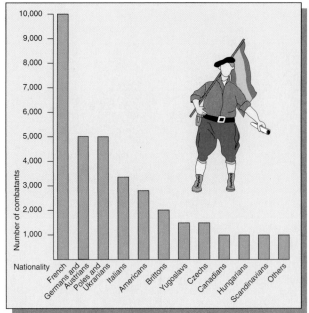

Churches desecrated and destroyed, monks' and priests' graves violated; such was the Socialist and Communist revenge for the support the Church gave to the Falangists. Understandable though they may be, such acts made a deep impact on Catholic public opinion. The violated graveyard of the *Convento des Magdalenas* in Barcelona.

German and Italian bomber planes supported Franco's troops by bombing Spanish cities held by the Republicans, such as Madrid. In other European countries people were appalled at the news of this active military support from abroad, witness this French poster (1937).

making it the idealized epic event of a popular and proletarian resistance against Fascist aggression. Militarily the result was disastrous. The Revolution destroyed the Republican Army, which was replaced by irregular badly disciplined forces based on militia of parties and trade unions led by untrained officers. The enthusiasm of the militia without doubt hindered the success of the rising. Until the spring of 1937 the Republic was unable to form a proper operational army. This was the prime reason for its defeat.

The advance on Madrid

The first objective of the rebels was Madrid. By the end of September 1936 the troops of the African Army commanded by Franco were at the southern outskirts of the capital after having advanced over 300 miles they had occupied a large part of the south and west of Spain and had taken important cities such as Badajoz and Toledo. Mola's troops had taken San Sebastian and the border country between the Basque Country and France and threatened Madrid from the mountains to the north of the city. The War was still only on a small scale. It was basically a war of columns in which both armies used few men. The infantry played the major role while the artillery, Air Force and Navy only played a small part. Nevertheless, one of the more sinister and cruel aspects of the War had already been seen. From the very beginning both sides repressed those left behind their lines on a large scale. Rebel troops shot members of the Left wing parties and trade unions, hundreds of teachers – a symbol of Republican secularism – certain Republican intellectuals (the best known of whom being García Lorca) and 16 priests with Basque Nationalism leanings. The Republicans, who were often no more than groups of assassins with no leader, executed those known for their Conservative and Catholic views, militants of the Right wing parties, military suspects, many priests and people in religious orders (6,500 in all during the war). Badajoz, where the Nationalists shot between 2,000 and 4,000 people in August 1936, and the radio

Acts of terror, committed on both sides, were the hallmark of the Spanish Civil War. At Amorabieta (Vizcaya) the 'reds' demolished civilian houses to intimidate the local population.

broadcasts of General Queipo de Llano from Seville were symbols of the violence of the supporters of Franco. The attacks on the prisons in Madrid and Bilbao and the shootings at Paracuellos del Jarama, near Madrid, were examples of the Republican terror. During the War a total of some 60,000 people were executed in the Franco area and at least 30,000 in the Republican area.

The attack on Madrid began in October 1936 and occupied several stages, all of which involved fierce fighting. Franco did not give up until February 1937 when his troops were held in the battle round the river Jarama. The resistance by Madrid, led by a Defense Council headed by General Miaja, reinforced the legend of Spanish anti-Fascism. It also demonstrated two other points – that the Republic was beginning to organize its armies and that the War was becoming internationalized. The former was made possible after the formation at the beginning of September of a Coalition Government headed by the Socialist Francisco Largo Caballero (1869-1946) in which the Communists held two posts and shortly afterwards four anarchist ministers were appointed. For the defense of Madrid Miaja had, as well as other troops, eight newly

The *Alcazar* of Toledo was held by the Falangists until it fell after a 70-day siege by the Republicans in 1937. This splendid fortress, built by Emperor Charles V, was utterly reduced to rubble. An exceptionally cruel repressive campaign followed its fall.

Inspection of the troops and salute to the Falangist flag (c. 1937).

The Republicans destroyed the Isabel II bridge in Bilbao to gain time on the advancing Falangists.

created brigades, two of them consisting of members of the International Brigades. He also had the use of Russian tanks and aircraft. Franco had German and Italian aircraft and armored cars. The efforts made by the United Kingdom and France to prevent international intervention in Spain and thus localize the conflict had failed. Germany and Italy recognized Franco in November 1936. During the same month Germany sent the Condor Legion and about 100 aircraft with pilots under German command, while some 5,000 advisers were sent during the 3 years' war. Italy sent some 70,000 troops which commenced fighting in January 1937. The USSR made some 2,000 advisers (instructors, pilots, gunners, etc.) available to the Republic. The International Brigades numbered about 60,000 men in all. Franco received some 1,200 German and Italian aircraft and about 350 tanks. The Republic received 1,300 aircraft and 900 tanks, almost all from the Soviet Union. The infantry war of the summer of 1936 was about to become a total war between two increasingly better equipped and larger armies – about 500,000 soldiers on each side in the spring of 1937. From then on the bombing and shelling of civilians was as important as fighting by the infantry.

Franco's successes

After the final, and again unsuccessful, offensive from Guadalajara against Madrid in March 1937, principally by Italian troops (4 divisions, 35,000 men, aircraft, tanks, etc.) Franco took the war to the north. On March 31, after very heavy bombardment by aircraft and artillery, he launched a major attack on the Basque Country, an autonomous region governed by a Nationalist Basque Government. On April 26 German aircraft destroyed Guernica, the spiritual capital of the Basques, an event which upset many people abroad. Bilbao, the principal city of the region, center of the steel industry, a Spanish naval base and the first port in the country, surrendered on June 19 after very heavy fighting. Several days later Franco achieved another major success; this time a moral and psychological victory. On July 1, 48 bishops publicized a document supporting the military uprising. The War was thus legitimized as a crusade defending religion. In spite of a brilliant Republican counterattack at Brunete near Madrid planned by the new Head of the Republican General Staff, General Vicente Rojo (1894-1966), Franco, who reacted in time and held the attack, took Santander in August and Asturias in October, with the result that he controlled the whole Cantabrian coast and the principal mining and steel-making centers in the country, a deciding factor in the ultimate victory.

In addition, on October 1, 1936, the Revolution General Staff appointed Franco Head of the Government, the State and Nationalist Spain. Franco wanted to create a new State, according to him based on totalitarianism and authority, a united, strong State and without autonomous regions; a military dictatorship with no political parties guided by the doctrines of the Catholic Church. In April 1937 he ordered all the political forces which had supported the uprising (Falangists, Catholics, Monarchists and Traditionalists) to be amalgamated into a single party. In January 1938 he set up his first Government and in April he proclaimed the *Fuero del Trabajo*, a type of founding charter for the new State, which was defined as a 'National-Syndicalist' regime, based on both Catholicism and Fascism.

Franco had introduced a single command in his area, a factor of decisive importance for the outcome of the War. This was in stark contrast to the policy changes in the Republican area. An anarchist Council or Government governed in Aragon from July 1936. From that time there were virtually two authorities in

The Red Terror

The Brest-Litowsk Pact did not bring peace to Russia. Although the Bolsheviks (renamed the Communist party in 1918) had eliminated the Provisional Government during the revolution, lack of discipline, food shortages and opposition from czarist reactionaries, liberals, the middle classes, constitutional democrats and anti-Leninist socialists (Mensheviks and Social Revolutionaries) gave rise to a (three-year) civil war. The economic policy of wartime Communism resulted in the expropriation of farmers' property. In addition, Japan and the Allies of Western Europe saw an opportunity to nip Communism in the bud. They not only supported the 'White' armies within Russia, but they themselves fought against the newly formed Red Army (lead by Leon Trotsky) along the western border (Ukraine, Armenia, Azerbaijzan until 1919) and the (north) eastern border (Archangel, Vladivostok until 1922). However, the diversity of anti-Bolshevik forces and their objectives was their weakness, while the Bolsheviks could appeal to patriotic feelings to fight against the Allies. Along with that, they also made effective use of propaganda and terror.

On December 7, 1917, only six weeks after the Russian Revolution, the Bolshevik regime created the Special Commission for the Fight against Contra-revolution and Sabotage, known by the abbreviation Vecheka, or Cheka for short. The name was changed several times later on (OGPU, NKVD, MVD, KGB), but the nature of the organization remained the same. It was a ramified political police force whose task it was to eliminate opponents of the Revolution by any means necessary. In the December 22, 1917, issue of *Pravda*, Lenin stated, 'The state is an instrument which upholds the power of the people. We want organized violence in the name of the interests of the workers.' Headed by chairman Felix Dzerzhinski, a tribunal was set up to try all enemies of the State. The first death sentence was pronounced in June of 1918. After attempts were made on the lives of Lenin and other leaders, the Red Terror decree was implemented. The decree empowered the Cheka to put class enemies into concentration camps and to execute enemies of the State. A wave of executions was the result, not always after summary trials. The murder of hostages was also the order of the day. During the summer of 1918, the peasants' revolts against grain expropriation were crushed. Czar Nicholas II and his family were murdered in Yekaterinenburg in July. Prisons, concentration camps and, from 1919 on, work camps were packed with strikers and political opponents who faced interrogation, torture and mass executions. In the words of Dzerzhinski's lieutenant Martin Latsis: 'We do not make war against individuals. We are exterminating the bourgeoisie as a class.'

Although the Communist state power was eventually successfully consolidated, estimates of the number of deaths vary from 50 to 150 thousand. In addition, more than two million highly educated people emigrated to the West to escape the regime. Due to this, the wounds left by the civil war took a long time to heal.

The Bolshevist 'Red' Terror held more than its own in comparison with the crimes perpetrated by the Whites. The Bolshevist *Cheka* (founded in 1917), the dreaded secret police, arrested thousands of people. In the period between 1918 and the first half of 1919 at least 8,389 persons were executed without trial in the Russian provinces alone. The Red Army and the *Cheka* were the twin pillars on which the Bolshevist victory in the civil war was built. In November 1920 the Red Army celebrated its victory over all the White generals in the streets of Moscow. On this occasion Trotsky and Stalin received the Order of the Red Banner for their efforts.

Catalonia – the Generalitat, the autonomous regional government made up of Catalan Left wingers, anarchists and Communists, and the powerful Catalan Central Committee of Anti-Fascist Militia led by the CNT, the anarchist Syndicalist trade union which controlled factories, supplies and the militia. The Central Republican Government's authority there was non-existent. A civil war within the Civil War broke out in May 1937 when militia of the CNT and POUM (Marxist Unification Workers Party), a small pro-Trotskyist party, opposed the Generalitat public order forces. The revolt was put down, but at a very high political and moral price. Largo Caballero resigned – he did not want the POUM to be outlawed – and was replaced by a new Government headed by another Socialist, Dr. Juan Negrin (1892-1952), in which the Communists held the key to power, possibly because it was they who understood best that total political and military unification of the Republicans was essential for a successful outcome to the War. The authority of

Several political groups had their own private armies, militias which roved the country, leaving death and destruction in their wake. View of the town of Belchite (Zaragoza) completely destroyed in 1936.

Refugees would on occasion stay in churches for weeks for want of better shelter.

the Central Government in Catalonia, and shortly afterwards in Aragon, was reaffirmed. Another situation emerged under the romantic vision of resistance to Fascism by Republican Spain – the gradual penetration of the political and military power apparatus of the Republicans by Communists. The Revolution had been betrayed for those who, like George Orwell a volunteer in the POUM militia, had idealized the proletarian nature of the struggle in Spain. Orwell, like other members of the POUM accused of being Fascist *agent provocateurs*, had to flee persecution by the police who were controlled by the Communist party.

The battle of the Ebro: the final victory

The Republicans launched another major counteroffensive in December 1937 and recaptured Teruel. However, the Nationalists re-took the city on February 22, the following year, and in March launched a major offensive along the Ebro Valley towards the Mediterranean, the beaches of which they reached on April 15 cutting the Republican territory in two. Franco then made the error of sending his armies towards Valencia in the south through exceptionally difficult country, the Maestrazgo Sierras, a move which aided the Republican defense. It was an operation which led to serious military complications, in spite of the fact that by then – the spring and summer of 1938 – he had achieved air and naval superiority. The Republican Navy had to spend most of its time in its ports; the supply of arms

The worst excesses of the war were perpetrated behind the front lines, where the civilian population was terrorized by death squads from the Left and the Right. Trenches around Azuara (Zaragoza).

and war materials by the USSR to the Republic via the Mediterranean had been seriously affected.

However, the Republic had still not been defeated. The Government of the energetic Negrin had improved the discipline of the People's Army and reorganized its troops effectively. Rojo again surprised Franco by his strategy. On July 25, 1938, the Republican Army crossed the river Ebro at several points and advanced in depth, threatening to break the Nationalist line. However, Franco again reacted in time, moving his armies to hold the Republican advance. Then, on August 11 he began an exhausting campaign to wear down the enemy's positions by making successive frontal attacks, the object of which was the final destruction of the People's Army. The battle of the Ebro was the most bitter and devastating of the War: 20,000 men died, and about 60,000 were missing from each side. Although the Republican Army still held Catalonia, Madrid, a large part of La Mancha, Valencia and southwest Spain and had an army of four large corps and a total of 49 divisions (8 less than Franco), the outcome of the War had been

Thousands of female Socialists and Communists took an active part in the Spanish Civil War. Girls from youth organizations in particular defended their ideals at the front. 'In the trenches' is a painting by Jésus Molina. Soldiers are reading a newspaper and a woman is mending clothes during a rare moment of peace.

Socialist solidarity demonstration for the Spanish Republic in
La Louvière, Belgium (August 14, 1938). The 'International Brigades', made
up of foreign idealists, fought on the side of the lawful government
of Spain. The Soviet Union also supported the Republican cause.
France and Great Britain remained neutral.

By 1938 Franco had defeated all but a few pockets of resistance.
On April 1, 1939, the *Falange* became the only national party, signalling a
nationwide campaign of repression. Falangists marching through
the streets of Madrid in a victory parade (March 28, 1939).

decided. The battle of the Ebro had destroyed the
morale and the ability of the People's Army to operate.

On December 10 Franco began the offensive against
Catalonia, one of the most brilliant military operations
he had commanded during the War. The result was the
swift collapse of Catalonia, with hardly any resistance. This angered President Azaña, who always
thought that Catalonia had not made enough contribu-

tion to the war effort (which although partly true was
also unjust – Barcelona, for example, suffered about
500 air raids during the War). Barcelona fell on
January 26, 1939 and a few days later Franco's troops
arrived at the French border. 500,000 people went into
exile, among them the President of the Republic,
Azaña, and General Vicente Rojo.

Only Negrin and his Communist advisers believed
that they could continue resisting, although, in view of
the state of both armies and the international situation
– as illustrated by the desire of the Western democracies to pacify Hitler and Mussolini, the principal pro-
tectors of Franco – it was probably impossible. In any
case, on March 4 Lieutenant Colonel Casado, Commander of the Army of the Center and apparent head
of the defeatist and non-Communist sector of the
Republic, rose against Negrin and formed a National
Defense Council to negotiate peace with Franco. For
several days Madrid was the scene of violent skir-
mishes between the troops of Casado and those of
Negrin, as a result of which about 2,000 people were
killed. In addition, Franco did not want any negotiation. He wanted unconditional surrender. His troops
entered Madrid on March 28, 1939, and on the 30th
they occupied Alicante, the last free Republican city
in whose port some 15,000 people were waiting in
vain to flee by sea. On April 1 Franco proclaimed victory. The War was over. In all about 300,000 people
had died, some 140,000 at the front and the remainder
behind the lines of both sides. 300,000 people went
into exile and another 300,000 were imprisoned by
Franco between 1939 and 1945 (it was estimated that
between 28,000 and 200,000 were executed during
this period). It was impossible to calculate the value
of buildings, bridges, railways, roads, ships, crops and
livestock destroyed. The period from 1939 to 1942
was a time of hunger for the people of Spain.

Creation of the 1931 Republic had been the most serious effort in the history of Spain to introduce modern
democracy to the country. Franco (1892-1975), a
small prudent expressionless man, a conservative
Catholic army officer, who believed that Liberalism
and political parties had been the cause of the troubles
in Spain, created an authoritarian regime with him as
dictator which lasted until he died. The new regime
was influenced by three factors: the Fascist and
Nationalist ideas of the Falange; the social/conserva-
tive thought of the Catholic Church; and the principles
of order, unity and authority of the military. Franco's
regime was initially totalitarian, clearly aligned with
the Germany of Hitler and the Italy of Mussolini.
From 1945 it was defined as a social and Catholic
monarchy – although there was no king on the throne.
It was only from the period from 1957 to 1961, after
two decades of Nationalist economy which brought
the country to the verge of bankruptcy, that the Franco
regime freed the economy and began the transforma-
tion which was to make Spain a modern, urban, industrial country. Democracy was restored after the death
of Franco on November 20, 1975. The question whether or not the Civil War of 1936-1939 was an unnecessary tragedy will forever recur in the history of Spain.

IN  FOCUS

A NATO exercise on Sicily.

War and peace in people's lives

1. Refugees from the former Yugoslavia arrive in Utrecht by train.
2. People demonstrating in Riga.
3. Visitors to the former concentration camp Auschwitz.
4. The start of a NATO conference in Vienna.
5. War commemoration in Rotterdam.
6. Passersby in front of an arms store in Paris.
7. A Russian commemorates his brothers who perished in the war.
8. A grieving family at the cemetery in Sarajevo.
9. A Dutch soldier leaves for the Gulf War.
10. The tomb of the unknown soldier in Paris.
11. A demonstrator warns against nuclear warfare.
12. Rape victims from Bosnia ask for justice.

7

8

9

10

11

12

1. A mournful procession of war invalids in Srebrnica.
2. International arms merchants close a deal in Paris.
3. Italian soldiers in action against organized crime.
4. A woman leaves a Bosnian mortuary in tears: her husband has been killed in the war.
5. A soldier offers help, Italy.
6. A young girl selling Nazi badges at a market, Cracow.
7. Red Cross staff at work in Sarajevo.
8. Former Venetian reinforcements on Rhodes.
9. A boy playing a war game on his computer.
10. Georgian soldiers go to church before battle.
11. Harsh reality in a trench in Abkhazia.

6

9

10 11

7

8

1

2

1. Demonstrators against emerging racism in Germany.
2. A woman visits the war cemetery in Gallipoli, Turkey.
3. Endless rows of crosses in a Dutch war cemetery.
4. Veterans commemorate World War II in Moscow.
5. Inhabitants of Sarajevo risking their lives to fetch water.
6. World War II commemoration in Poland.
7. A British soldier stares at the destruction caused by a bomb attack in Belfast.
8. Victims of German concentration camps from World War II.
9. The ruins of a castle in Valkenburg, the Netherlands.
10. The destruction following heavy fighting in Croatia.
11. A Russian soldier on guard.
12. A young boy gaping at the latest fighters.

3

4

5

6

7

8

9

10

11

12

IN FOCUS

1. Hardly anyone dares to appear on the streets of the besieged city of Sarajevo.
2. Greek soldiers in action during a NATO exercise.
3. Fleeing from the war in the former Yugoslavia, women and children find refuge in a sports hall in Split.
4. Amnesty International stands up for political prisoners.
5. Mass protest against nuclear weapons in Amsterdam.

1

2

3

4

5

HISTORICAL FILE

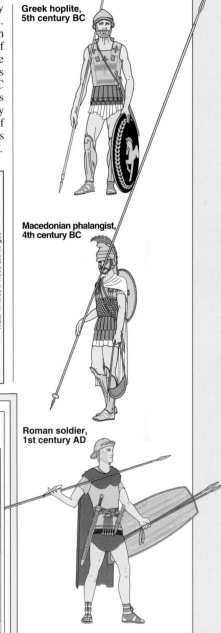

Greek hoplite,
5th century BC

Macedonian phalangist,
4th century BC

Roman soldier,
1st century AD

WAR IN ANTIQUITY

Weapons and Combat Troops

For many centuries, the spear was the most important of all weapons used for fighting in Greek and Latin antiquity. Use of the spear promoted the formation of a closed fighting unit, the *phalanx*. The shapes of spears and protective shields varied in different times and places. Greek *hoplites* wore big, round shields.

But Macedonian *phalangists* could put their small shields on their backs, freeing both hands to use their 14.5 foot (4.5 meters) long stabbing spears. Roman legionaries had flat shields and three javelins at their disposal. For the Romans, the sword became the main weapon.

Also in antiquity, keeping an army going required sound logistics. Every soldier had to get enough calories to endure long days of marching and battle. Alexander the Great's army conquered large parts of Asia and Africa between 334 BC and 320 BC. It is estimated that this huge army needed approximately 495,000 pounds (225,000 kg) of grain and about 158,400 gallons (720,000 liters) of water every day.

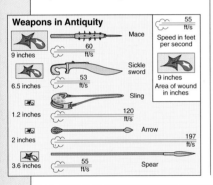

Weapons in Antiquity

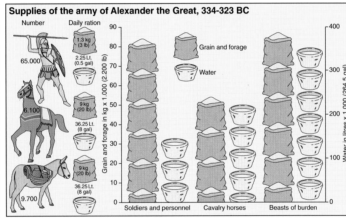

Supplies of the army of Alexander the Great, 334-323 BC

The Roman Army

The highest ranks in the Roman army were held by the aristocratic senators and *equites* (knights). A 6,000-man legion was commanded by six tribunes, one of whom was a senator and the other five knights. Usually, these commanders were between 30 and 45 years old and their pay ranged from 50,000 to 500,000 sesterces a year. Regular infantrymen could rise to the rank of *centurion* (hundredman); each legion had about 60 of these. These relatively old hands (their minimum age was 50) were the legion's professional core.

Equestrian officers of the Roman imperial army, 27 BC-268 AD

	Age in years	Salary in sesterces
SENATOR		
Commander; Governor of an important province	min. 41	500,000
Governor of a less important province	min. 30	300,000
Commander of a legion in an important province	c. 30	200,000
CANDIDATE FOR SENATOR		
Staff officer of the commander	16-24	80,000
EQUITES		
Officers with administrative tasks	35-45	50,000
REGULAR OFFICERS		
Technical commander of the legion	min. 55	120,000
Camp commander	min. 51	80,000
Commander of the first cohort	min. 50	60,000
Centurion	min. 50	30-50,000

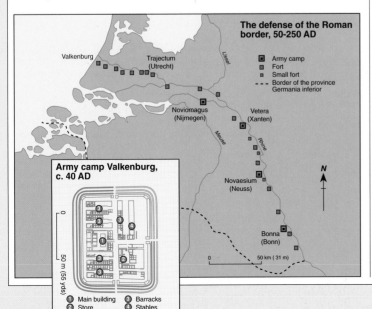

Army camp Valkenburg, c. 40 AD
① Main building ③ Barracks
② Store ④ Stables

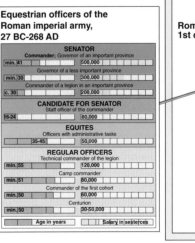

The defense of the Roman border, 50-250 AD
■ Army camp
■ Fort
■ Small fort
-- Border of the province Germania inferior

Border Defense on the Lower Rhine

Emperor Augustus (30 BC-14 AD) expanded the Roman Empire to the Danube and the Rhine. From then on the army's objective was to defend the empire; the legions (Roman legionaries) and auxiliaries (soldiers from the provinces) were stationed in army camps and forts along the river borders. They were to protect the Empire from invasion by Germanic tribes. The fort in *Valkenburg*, built during Emperor Claudius' reign (41 - 54 AD), was situated near the Rhine estuary. This fort measured 351 by 429 feet (108 by 132 meters); it could accommodate one cohort (600 soldiers) and was enclosed by an earthen wall with a stockade and three moats. The fort was rebuilt four times and was deserted for good in 250 AD.

137

WAR IN THE MIDDLE AGES

The Medieval Florentine Cavalry

In the Middle Ages, the term 'mercenary' was not a pejorative as it is today. There was no such thing as conscription and therefore no homogenous, 'national' army, so practically every ruler hired 'foreign' soldiers. The table shows, for example, that in 1325 only one fourth of Florence's cavalrymen really were of Florentine origin.

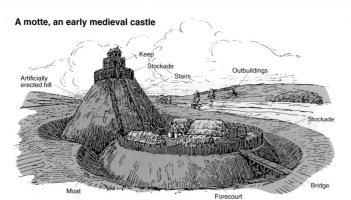

The Florentine cavalry, 1325

Florentines
French
Germans
Catalans
Italians, Flemings and others

Number of cavalrymen
0   100   200   300   400   500   600   700

Fighting and Earning

Soldiers earned relatively high wages. In France, skilled laborers usually earned twice as much as unskilled workers. If these unskilled workers threw in their lot with the state army, their future could look considerably brighter; in years when the demand for soldiers was high, for instance in 1380, these men could earn even more than skilled construction workers. Medieval cities were generally easy to defend. The city walls, often complemented by a moat, formed a

Salary of a foot-soldier in France, 1320-1500

Pennies

Construction worker
Foot-soldier

70
60
50
40
30
20
10
0
1320 1350 1380 1410 1440 1470 1500

closed, protective belt around the city. During an attack, the citizens could take cover behind the wall or in one of the various towers. This high, strategic vantage point meant the defending party required far fewer weapons than the attackers, who usually had to approach the city from open fields. But the attackers' cannons and catapults were still capable of doing great damage to the besieged city.

Defending and attacking a medieval city

Crossbows
Bows
Arrows
Battle axes
Large catapults
Stones
Guns
Lead
Gunpowder

Defenders
Attackers

Ratio defenders : attackers
0 1 2 3 4 5 6 7 8 9 10 11 12 13 14 15 16 17 18 19 20

Destruction by War

France was the battlefield of the Hundred Years' War. This feudal and dynastic conflict between England and France continued, on and off, for 116 years.

This map shows which areas were the bones of contention between the two countries, and consequently suffered most from the war: Guyenne in Southern France, Picardie and Artois in the Northwest. England won the major battles that are indicated on this map. But eventually, the English kings had to give up their claims to the French throne and various French regions.

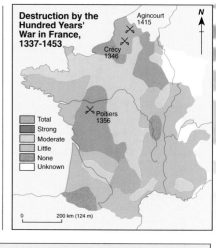

Destruction by the Hundred Years' War in France, 1337-1453

Agincourt 1415
Crécy 1346
Poitiers 1356

Total
Strong
Moderate
Little
None
Unknown

0   200 km (124 mi)

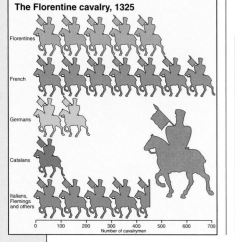

A motte, an early medieval castle

Keep
Stockade
Stairs
Outbuildings
Artificially erected hill
Stockade
Moat
Forecourt
Bridge

A Feudal Fortress

For a feudal lord it was important to build his stronghold and court on an elevated piece of land; in this way, he 'ruled over' the surrounding area and he was better protected from attack. If nature had not been kind enough to provide a natural elevation (for example, on a plain), an artificial mound, known as a *motte*, was raised. On this motte, a lord would build his refuge stronghold, which in the early Middle Ages was usually no more than a wooden tower. Often there was a forecourt close to the motte, which accommodated a manor house and farm. Both refuge stronghold and forecourt were protected by a moat and palisade.

The Cross Bow

As early as the classical age, the cross bow had been developed from the longbow. This weapon consisted of a short, strong bow fixed across a wooden shaft. In comparison with the longbow, the advantage of the cross bow was its capacity to shoot heavier arrows. And it had a much longer range; by the end of the fifteenth century, an arrow shot from a cross bow could travel 1140 feet (350 meters). But reloading was far more time-consuming; only one or two arrows could be shot per minute.

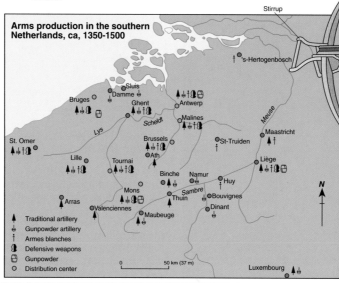

Medieval crossbow

Stirrup
Roller
Shaft
String
Trigger

Arms production in the southern Netherlands, ca. 1350-1500

's-Hertogenbosch
Sluis
Damme
Bruges
Ghent
Antwerp
Malines
Scheldt
Lys
St. Omer
Brussels
Maastricht
St-Truiden
Lille
Tournai
Liège
Ath
Binche
Namur
Mons
Huy
Thuin
Sambre
Bouvignes
Arras
Dinant
Valenciennes
Maubeuge
Luxembourg

Meuse

Traditional artillery
Gunpowder artillery
Armes blanches
Defensive weapons
Gunpowder
Distribution center

0   50 km (37 mi)

N

Weapons Production

In the late Middle Ages, the Southern Low Countries were an important European arms manufacturing center, because the raw materials (iron ore and wood to heat the blast-furnaces) needed were mined in the Sambre and Meuse valleys. Also, the international markets in Bruges and Antwerp provided excellent sales potential. The main centers were in Tournai, Mons, Malines, Bruges and Antwerp.

REVOLTS IN EARLY MODERN EUROPE

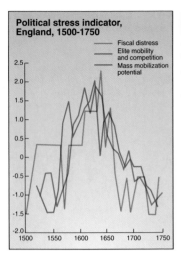

Political stress indicator, England, 1500-1750

- Fiscal distress
- Elite mobility and competition
- Mass mobilization potential

Internal Strife

In the sixteenth and seventeenth centuries, civil strife was rampant in almost all of Western Europe. One interesting theory suggests that the Civil War in England (1642-1648), for example, was caused by a concurrence of tension in several fields in society. In the entire period from 1500 to 1640, government finance, stability in the ruling class-

es and employment were under tremendous pressure because of the explosive population growth and the resulting inflation. The combination of factors such as tax burden, mobility of the elite and the ability to mobilize the popular masses can be referred to as an 'political stress indicator'. If these three factors are quantified, all of them appear to have increased in the first half of the seventeenth century. Against this background, an event like the civil war seemed almost inevitable.

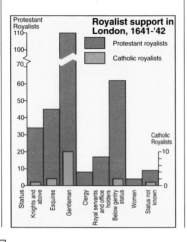

Royalist support in London, 1641-'42

- Protestant royalists
- Catholic royalists

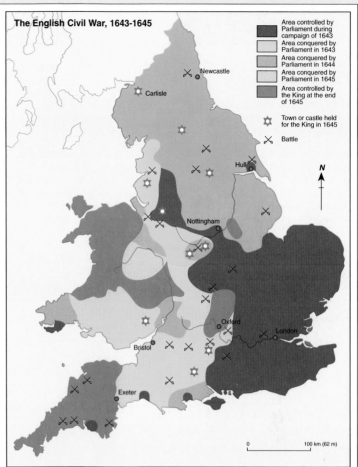

The English Civil War, 1643-1645

- Area controlled by Parliament during campaign of 1643
- Area conquered by Parliament in 1643
- Area conquered by Parliament in 1644
- Area conquered by Parliament in 1645
- Area controlled by the King at the end of 1645
- ✶ Town or castle held for the King in 1645
- ✕ Battle

0   100 km (62 m)

The Warring Factions in the Civil War

Simplistic explanations can hardly clarify drastic events like the English Civil War. For example, supporters of English King Charles I (1625-1649) who were arrested in London were of different social classes and religious backgrounds, although they were predominantly noble-

men. However, their support of the King was to no avail. In the many battles that were fought in this war, more and more territory was lost to the Parliament faction. The Civil War ended in 1649 when the King was executed and the monarchy was abolished. It was restored in 1660 with the accession to the throne of King Charles II (1660-1685).

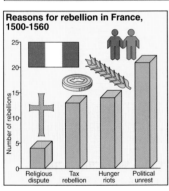

Reasons for rebellion in France, 1500-1560

- Religious dispute
- Tax rebellion
- Hunger riots
- Political unrest

Social Unrest in France

In the sixteenth and seventeenth centuries, France was struggling with the same kind of problems as England. There too, the tax burden, rising food prices and government restrictions on traditional political rights led the population to revolt against the authorities. Religious tension, combined with conflicts over succession to the throne until 1653, also caused wide social unrest. The French kings continually felt the need to assert their authority ever more emphatically throughout the country. This often met with resistance in the provinces, which feared their regional autonomy would crumble. That is why, in the sixteenth and seventeenth centuries, the monarch regularly took harsh measures.

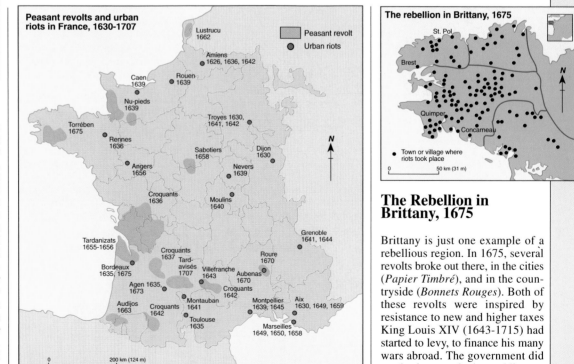

Peasant revolts and urban riots in France, 1630-1707

- Peasant revolt
- Urban riots

The rebellion in Brittany, 1675

- Town or village where riots took place

0   50 km (31 m)

The Rebellion in Brittany, 1675

Brittany is just one example of a rebellious region. In 1675, several revolts broke out there, in the cities (*Papier Timbré*), and in the countryside (*Bonnets Rouges*). Both of these revolts were inspired by resistance to new and higher taxes King Louis XIV (1643-1715) had started to levy, to finance his many wars abroad. The government did not hesitate to deploy soldiers to quash these revolts.

FORTIFICATIONS

Defense of Cities and Countryside

The appearance of European cities changed over the course of time. In the late Middle Ages, a city was encircled by a high, narrow, loopholed wall with small towers. In the sixteenth century, these city walls were replaced or supplemented by a thick wall with broad, round turrets that could accommodate artillery. In the seventeenth century, fortifica-tion was on the rise: the turrets were replaced by bastions, pentangular fortifications of Italian origin. From the bastion's two long sides, the enemy could be fought with heavy artillery. From its flanks, the two sides perpendicular to the long sides, the wall between two bastions could be defended. For the same purpose, there were defense works in the moat: triangular rave-lins. In the course of the seven-teenth century, another two fortifications rose outside the moat: a hornwork and a crownwork.

In 1568 the provinces in the North-ern Low Countries rose in revolt against their sovereign, Philip II (1156-1598), who was also king of Spain. During this Eighty Years' War (1568-1648), many cities in the Northern Low Countries were turned into fortresses. During an assault, the surrounding areas could be flooded to prevent enemy armies from besieging the city. In 1672, the so-called 'year of disaster', the province of Holland even succeed-ed in stopping the onslaught of French troops by flooding a nearly unbroken strip of land from the Zuiderzee to the delta of Zeeland. This strip became known as the *Hollandse Waterlinie*.

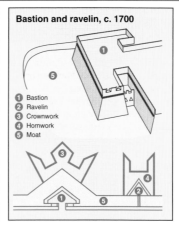

Bastion and ravelin, c. 1700

1. Bastion
2. Ravelin
3. Crownwork
4. Hornwork
5. Moat

Defensive works, 1400-1700

Medieval city wall, c. 1400   Wall with round turrets, c. 1550   Fortifications, c. 1700

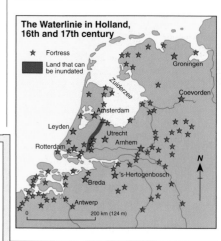

The Waterlinie in Holland, 16th and 17th century

★ Fortress

▇ Land that can be inundated

Groningen, Coevorden, Zuiderzee, Amsterdam, Leyden, Utrecht, Arnhem, Rotterdam, 's-Hertogenbosch, Breda, Antwerp

0   200 km (124 m)   N

THE ARSENALS

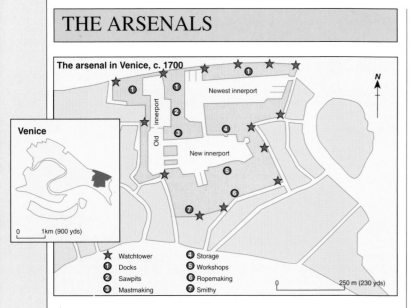

The arsenal in Venice, c. 1700

Newest innerport
Old innerport
New innerport
N

Venice

0   1km (900 yds)

★ Watchtower
1 Docks
2 Sawpits
3 Mastmaking
4 Storage
5 Workshops
6 Ropemaking
7 Smithy

0   250 m (230 yds)

city-state in the eighteenth century. The center of power had moved from southern Europe northwards. The new naval powers, the Low Countries, England and France, possessed many overseas territo-ries, both in Asia and the America's. They needed warships to protect and expand their empires. England surpassed them all with a produc-tion level sometimes approaching 90 ships per decade. This was for example, the case in the periods 1741-1750 and 1781-1790.

In coastal towns, the arsenals pro-vided many people with a living. In the late eighteenth century, some 15 to 16,000 men worked in the Spanish arsenals of Cadiz, Ferrol and Cartagena.

The advent of the steam engine and iron hulled ships in the nineteenth century gradually brought the pro-duction of relatively simple, wood-en sailing ships to an end. The traditional arsenals were ill-equipped for the manufacture of the new, much larger, iron steamships. As a result of this, employment dropped drastically.

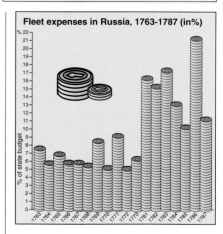

Fleet expenses in Russia, 1763-1787 (in%)

% of state budget

1763 ... 1787

A War Fleet for Russia

Czarina Catherine the Great (1762-1796) expanded the Russian empire with regions in the north (the Baltic states and part of Poland) and in the south (the Crimea on the Black Sea). In both regions, she put a high priority on building up a war fleet to fight the Swedes to the north and the Turks to the south. These fleet expenses cut deeply into the nation-al treasury; in 1786 for example, one year before the outbreak of the Russian-Turkish war of 1787-1791, more than a fifth of the total budget of Russia was spent on the fleet.

Warships Production

As early as the twelfth century, the city-state of Venice began to flour-ish politically and economically, and started building a large naval arsenal. This *arsenale vecchio*, where ships were built and equipped, was expanded several times in the centuries to follow. The Venetian arsenal saw its glory decline with the fall of the Italian

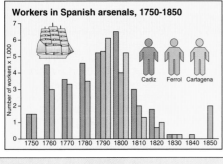

Workers in Spanish arsenals, 1750-1850

Number of workers x 1,000

Cadiz   Ferrol   Cartagena

1750 1760 1770 1780 1790 1800 1810 1820 1830 1840 1850

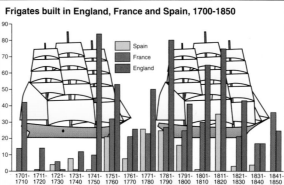

Frigates built in England, France and Spain, 1700-1850

▢ Spain
▦ France
▇ England

1701-1710 1711-1720 1721-1730 1731-1740 1741-1750 1751-1760 1761-1770 1771-1780 1781-1790 1791-1800 1801-1810 1811-1820 1821-1830 1831-1840 1841-1850

THE SPANISH CIVIL WAR

Disputing the History of Spain

In February 1936, the Spanish parliamentary elections were held. The Popular Front, a coalition of all left-wing parties, only just won the elections, but was soon divided by the question of how Spanish society should be changed; gradually, through the parliamentary process, or through revolution. Spain's conservative forces decided not to wait for an answer and joined forces to stem, in their eyes, the rising tide of communism. A few months after that a devastating civil war broke out.

During General Franco's regime, which lasted from 1939 to 1975, independent historical research about the civil war was strictly prohibited. Only the victors' version of events was accepted. Outside Spain, many works based on unreliable sources were published. This, for instance, is why nowadays there are at least eleven different versions of the February 1936 parliamentary election results. This changed gradually after Franco died, when the archives were opened to the public and more objective research became possible.

The elections in Spain, 1936

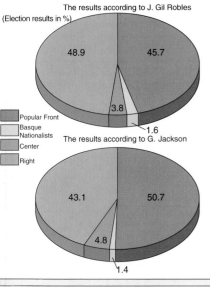

The results according to J. Gil Robles
(Election results in %)

- Popular Front
- Basque Nationalists
- Center
- Right

The results according to G. Jackson

Foreign (Non-)Intervention

France and England wanted to prevent the Spanish conflict from escalating into an international war. They managed to join 23 European countries and the United States in a Non-Intervention committee. This committee decided not to supply arms to the contending parties in Spain. From April 1937 onwards, German and Italian warships patrolled the coast of Republican Spain, while French and English warships patrolled the coast of Nationalist-controlled Spain to enforce compliance with the non-intervention pact. In practice, however, this effort failed. Hitler and Mussolini supplied Franco with huge amounts of weapons. They hoped to ensure him with a quick victory and thereby win themselves a new ally in Europe. The Republicans, on the other hand, received considerable military support from the Soviet Union. Historians still disagree on exactly how much weaponry was smuggled in, which is why it is only possible to come up with lowest and highest estimates.

Non-intervention naval patrol, 1937

Nationalist Spain

Republican Spain

German navy
Italian navy
French navy
British navy

0   200 km (124 m)

Foreign military assistance to Republicans and Nationalists, 1936-1939

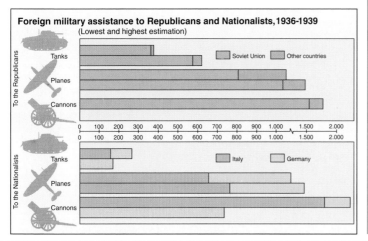

(Lowest and highest estimation)

To the Republicans: Tanks, Planes, Cannons — Soviet Union, Other countries

To the Nationalists: Tanks, Planes, Cannons — Italy, Germany

Financing the Spanish Civil War, 1936-1939

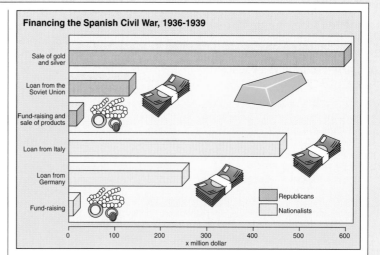

- Sale of gold and silver
- Loan from the Soviet Union
- Fund-raising and sale of products
- Loan from Italy
- Loan from Germany
- Fund-raising

Republicans
Nationalists

x million dollar

Funding for the War

In principle, those who represent state power in a civil war have the advantage. After all, they have easy access to the treasury. The Spanish Republicans, for example, financed the war by selling large amounts of gold and silver to the national banks of the Soviet Union, France and the United States. A collection among private citizens produced many jewels, gold coins and watches. The Nationalists also held such a collection. However, the proceeds were dwarfed by the loans Franco was granted by the fascist regimes in Italy and Germany.

The Spanish Battlefield

By April 1938, Franco's Nationalist troops reached the Ebro valley. This river and mountain area was Catalonia's and the Republicans' natural line of defense. Because Franco's armies first turned their attention to Valencia, Republican troops were able to recapture most of the Ebro valley. However, Franco once again captured the valley after a bloody battle in November 1938. Within two months, his army had conquered all of Catalonia.

The Nationalists and Republicans suffered about the same number of casualties on the battlefield. But not all the victims died in battle. Twice as many people died of disease and starvation. The Republican zones that were cut off from the outside world were much harder hit than Nationalist-controlled areas. Furthermore, executions of Spaniards with Republican sympathies continued well into the 1960s.

Battle of the Ebro, 1938

Front line on:
— 24 July
— 31 July
— 30 Oct.
— 16 Nov.

Ascó, Ebro, Gandesa, Benisanet, Benifollet, Cherta

0   8 km (5 m)

Battle of Catalonia, 1938-1939

Huesca, Lérida, Ebro, Segre, Figueras 8-2-'39, Gerona 4-3-'39, Tarragona 15-1-'39, Barcelona 22-1-'39, Fayón, Benifollet, Teruel

- Nationalist territory Dec. 1937
- Nationalist gains March - Apr. 1938
- Nationalist gains Apr.- Jul. 1938
- Nationalist gains Dec. 1938 - Jan. 1939
- Nationalist gains Jan. - Feb. 1939

0   50 km (26 m)

Deaths due to the Civil War, 1936-1961

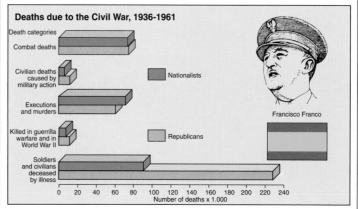

Death categories:
- Combat deaths
- Civilian deaths caused by military action
- Executions and murders
- Killed in guerrilla warfare and in World War II
- Soldiers and civilians deceased by illness

Nationalists
Republicans

Number of deaths x 1.000

Francisco Franco

INDUSTRIAL WARFARE

Large-scale War

Growing industrialization in the nineteenth century considerably increased the destructive power of armies. The greatly improved artillery were mass-produced. From then on, wars were no longer decided by short battles.

Armies took up positions and continuously bombarded the enemy. This made for example the battlefield along the river Somme during World War I much larger than the one in Waterloo in 1815.

In World War I every countries army had its own network of trenches. The British network, for example, had three parallel lines connected by perpendicular trenches. Usually, a 32.5 foot (10 meters) long barbed wire entanglement was put up about 65 feet (20 meters) in front of the front line in no man's land.

The front line was backed up by support troops and reinforcements in the second and third lines which could be sent to the front line whenever necessary. Between the lines, there were several small strongpoints, manned by light artillery units. The heavy artillery was placed behind the trench network.

Battlefield Survivors

Medical developments in the late nineteenth and early twentieth centuries increased the chances of survival for wounded soldiers. Anaesthesia made surgery and amputations less painful and antiseptics helped prevent infection. Still, warfare claimed many casualties. Some 850,000 soldiers were left handicapped by World War I. Wounds and amputations were the main causes of disability. But doctors could do very little for soldiers who returned home with psychological traumas caused by seeing the horrors of war.

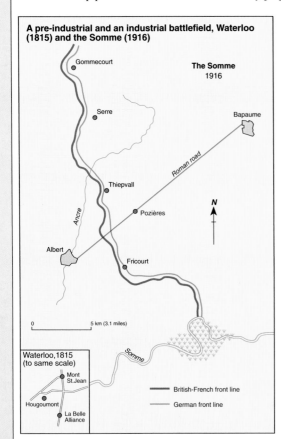

A pre-industrial and an industrial battlefield, Waterloo (1815) and the Somme (1916)

The Somme 1916

Gommecourt
Serre
Bapaume
Roman road
Thiepvall
Pozières
Ancre
Albert
Fricourt
Somme

0   5 km (3.1 miles)

Waterloo,1815 (to same scale)
Mont St.Jean
Hougoumont
La Belle Alliance

—— British-French front line
—— German front line

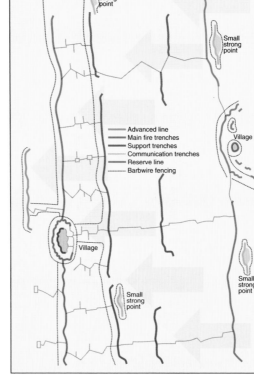

British trench system, 1914-1918

Small strong point
Small strong point
Village

— Advanced line
— Main fire trenches
— Support trenches
— Communication trenches
— Reserve line
-- Barbwire fencing

Village
Small strong point
Small strong point

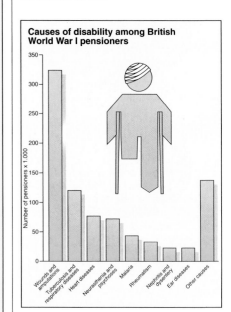

Causes of disability among British World War I pensioners

Number of pensioners x 1.000

Wounds and amputations
Tuberculosis and respiratory diseases
Heart diseases
Neurasthenia and psychoses
Malaria
Rheumatism
Nephritis and dysentery
Ear diseases
Other causes

The Casualties of the World Wars

The Second World War caused many more civilian casualties than the First World War. The Jews suffered the biggest losses; Hitler's *Endlösung* ('final solution' of the Jewish 'problem') meant the annihilation of over six million Jews, about half of whom were from Poland.

More than half of all the soldiers killed in action were Russian.

War and Working Women in Europe

During both World War I and World War II, the war industry in all of Europe was at full production capacity. Due to the mobilization of the male population, a great labor shortage, especially in the factories, arose. As a result of this, in many European countries, women had to be employed to fill the gap.

In Great Britain and Ireland, for example, the number of women working in industry grew by some 800,000 during World War I. By comparison, the number of women working in transportation and trade grew even faster.

During World War II, Germany however was less successful at getting women to work in its factories. In this country most of the working women were employed in the agrarian sector. Foreigners and prisoners of war were forced to work in the factories. They had to replace the German men who, as soldiers, no longer were available for the production process.

The female labor force in Great Britain and Ireland, 1914-1918

Sectors:
Transport
Catering industry
Agriculture
Government
Self-employed
Home work
Commerce
Industry

1914
1918

Number of women x 1.000   0   100 200 300 400 500 600 700 800 900 1.000 1.500 2.000 2.500 3.000

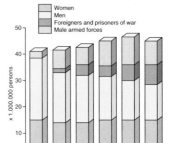

The composition of the German labor force, 1939-1944

□ Women
□ Men
■ Foreigners and prisoners of war
□ Male armed forces

x 1.000.000 persons

1939 1940 1941 1942 1943 1944

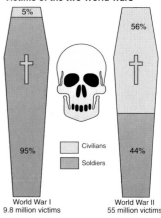

Victims of the two World Wars

5%
56%

□ Civilians
■ Soldiers

95%
44%

World War I
9.8 million victims

World War II
55 million victims

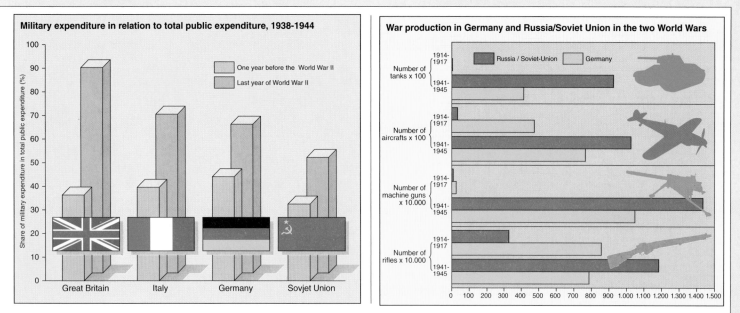

Military expenditure in relation to total public expenditure, 1938-1944

Share of military expenditure in total public expenditure (%)

One year before the World War II
Last year of World War II

Great Britain Italy Germany Sovjet Union

War production in Germany and Russia/Soviet Union in the two World Wars

Russia / Soviet-Union   Germany

Number of tanks x 100 — 1914-1917 / 1941-1945

Number of aircrafts x 100 — 1914-1917 / 1941-1945

Number of machine guns x 10.000 — 1914-1917 / 1941-1945

Number of rifles x 10.000 — 1914-1917 / 1941-1945

0 100 200 300 400 500 600 700 800 900 1.000 1.100 1.200 1.300 1.400 1.500

War Expenditure in the Twentieth Century

Industrial warfare takes up a large part of the national budget of present day countries. The manufacture of new, technologically advanced weaponry is very expensive. In addition, maintaining massive armies, and thus paying millions of soldiers is also extremely costly.

In World War II, European countries raised funds for the war by means of tax increases and national loans. In the 1930s, Germany succeeded in building up a huge war machine. In 1938, for example, it spent more than half of its total budget on the military. Britain's foreign policy at that time was one of appeasement. In this period before the outbreak of the war, a third of the national budget was spent on the armed forces. During the war, military spending grew exponentially: in 1944, 90% of the national budget went towards the war effort.

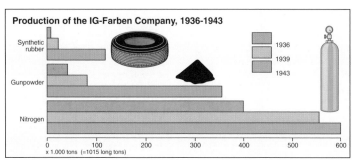

Production of the IG-Farben Company, 1936-1943

Synthetic rubber

Gunpowder

Nitrogen

1936
1939
1943

0 100 200 300 400 500 600
x 1.000 tons (=1015 long tons)

Production

Industrial capacity is crucial to a country's chance of winning a war. That is why the armies of the still largely agrarian Russia could not stand up to those of industrialized Germany in 1914. In the 1930s, Stalin's Five-Year Plans greatly stimulated industry of the Soviet Union. During World War II, the tables were turned and now the Soviet Union produced up to twice as many weapons as Germany.

Chemical Industry and Warfare

The wide use of chemicals in arms manufacturing made the warring nations increasingly dependent on chemical producers. The German army, the *Wehrmacht*, for instance, depended almost entirely on the production of the large *IG-Farben* company for its synthetic rubber, nitrogen and gunpowder. It is no wonder that production figures for these materials skyrocketed.

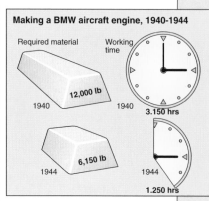

Making a BMW aircraft engine, 1940-1944

Required material   Working time

12,000 lb
1940   1940   3.150 hrs

6,150 lb
1944   1944   1.250 hrs

During World War II rationalization played an important role in Germany's production process. In the BMW plants, for instance the engineers managed to minimize both the materials and manhours needed for aircraft engine manufacturing. This in turn increased the output of this firm from 160 engines per month in 1940 to 360 per month in 1944.

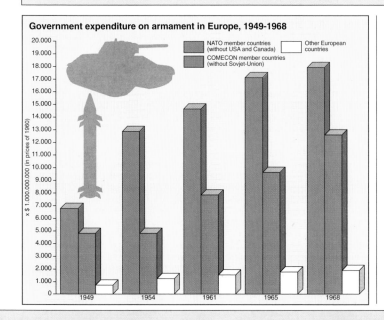

Government expenditure on armament in Europe, 1949-1968

x $ 1.000.000.000 (in prices of 1960)

NATO member countries (without USA and Canada)
COMECON member countries (without Sovjet-Union)
Other European countries

1949 1954 1961 1965 1968

Military Expenditure in the Cold War Era

After World War II, enmity arose between the Soviet Union and the United States. By means of military alliances, both nations quickly managed to win the allegiance of the European countries they had liberated.

The two blocs engaged in a *Cold War*: each side believed that possessing as many (nuclear) weapons as possible would deter the enemy from starting a war. Although the governments of both the United States and the Soviet Union paid most of the immense cost of the arms race, Europe also spent billions of dollars. In all European countries, military spending nearly tripled in the period between the years 1949 and 1968.

The end of the Cold War has allowed the United Nations to step up the number of peacekeeping missions. The multinational forces, also known as the *blue berets*, have increased in size in recent years.

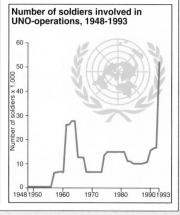

Number of soldiers involved in UNO-operations, 1948-1993

Number of soldiers x 1.000

1948 1950 1960 1970 1980 1990 1993

BIBLIOGRAPHY

General
Contamine, P. *La guerre au moyen age* (1980)
Parker, G. *The military revolution. Military innovation and the rise of the West, 1500-1800* (1988)
Anderson, M.S. *War and society in Europe of the Old Regime, 1618-1789* (1988)
Creveld, M. van *Supplying war* (1977)
Lindegren, J. *Utskrivning och utsugning (Conscription and exploitation)* (1980)
Lindegren, J. *The resources of the early modern state (preliminary title)* (1993)

War in the Greek and Roman world
Pritchett, W.K. *The Greek state at war I - V* (1971-1991)
Anderson, J.K. *Military theory and practice in the age of Xenophon* (1970)
Hanson, V. *The Western way of war. Infantry battle in Classical Greece* (1989)
Griffith, G.T. *The mercenaries of the Hellenistic world* (1968) (1935')
Launey, M. *Recherches sur les armées hellénistiques I - II* (1949-50)
Harmand, J. *L'armée et le soldat à Rome* (1957)
Keppie, L. *The making of the Roman army* (1984)
Le Bohec, Y. *L'armée romaine* (1989)
Luttwak, E.N. *The grand strategy of the Roman empire* (1976)
Ferrill, A. *The fall of the Roman empire; The military explanation* (1986)

Art of war in medieval Europe
Brown, R.A. *Castles, conquest and charters, collected papers* (1989)
Cardini, F. *La culture de la guerre, Xe-XVIIIe siècle* (1992)
Contamine, P. *La guerre au Moyen Age* (1992) 3e ed
Contamine, P. ed. *Des origines à 1715* (1992)
Demurger, A. *Vie et mort de l'ordre du Temple, 1118-1314* (1989)
Duby, G. *Le dimanche de Bouvines* (1973)
Fleckenstein, J. ed. *Das ritterliche Turnier im Mittelalter* (1985)
Flori, J. *L'essor de la chevalerie, XIe-XIIe siècles* (1986)
Keen, M. *Chivalry* (1984)
Schmidtchen, V. *Kriegswesen im späten Mittelalter. Technik, Taktik, Theorie* (1990)
Verbruggen, J.F. *The art of warfare in Western Europe during the Middle Ages* (1977)

Bastion fortifications
De la Croix, H. *Military considerations in city planning: fortifications* (1972)
'Palmanova: a study in sixteenth century urbanism' in: *Saggi e memorie di storia dell'arte* (1967)
De Seta, C. en J. Le Goff eds. *La città e le mura* (1989)
Guerlac, H. 'Vauban: the impact of science of war' in: P. Paret ed. *Makers of the modern strategy from Machiavelli to the nuclear age* (9186)
Guidoni Marino, A. 'L'architetto e la fortezza: qualità artistica e tecniche militari nel"500"' in: *Storia dell'arte italiana XII: Momenti di architectura* (1983)
Hale J.R. 'The early development of the bastion, an Italian chronology (c.1450-c.1534)' in: J.R. Hale, B. Smalley, J.R.L. Highfield eds. *Europe in the Late Middle Ages* (1985)
Hook, J. 'Fortifications and the end of Sienese state' in: *History LXII* (1977)
Kunisch J. ed. *Staatsverfassung und Heeresverfassung in der europäischen Geschichte der früher Neuzeit* (1986)
Lavedan, P. *Histoire de l'urbanisme. Renaissance et temps modernes* (1959) 2nd. ed.
Pepper, S. en N. Adams *Firearms and fortifications. Military architecture and siege warfare in 16th century Siena* (1986)
Schutte, U. ed. *Arkitekt und Ingenieur. Baumeister in Krieg und Frieden* (1984)

Collective violence
Bak, J., M. Benecke en G. Benecke eds. *Religion and rural revolt* (1984)
Bercé, Y.-M. *Histoire des croquants. Etude des soulèvements populaires au XVIIe siècle dans le sud-ouest de la France* (1974)
Bercé, Y.-M. *Croquants et Nu-Pieds. Les soulèvements paysans en France du XVIe au XIXe siècle* (1974)
Bercé, Y.-M. *Révoltes et révolutions dans l'Europe moderne* (1980)
Blockmans, W.P. 'La répression de révoltes urbaines comme méthode de centralisation dans les Pays-Bas bourguignons' in: *Rencontres de Milan (1er au 3me octobre 1987): Milan et les Etats bourguignons: deux ensembles politiques princiers entre Moyen Age et Renaissance (XIVe-XVIe s.)* (1988)
Brake, W. te *Revolt and religious reformation in the world of Charles V, 1516-1555* (1992)
Charlesworth, A. ed. *An atlas of rural protest in Britain 1548-1900* (1983)
Davies, C.S.L. 'Les révoltes populaires en Angleterre, 1500-

1700' in: *Annales; economies, sociétés, civilisation 24* (1969)
Davies, C.S.L. 'Peasant revolt in France and England: a comparison' in: *Agricultural history review 21* (1973)
Dekker, R. *Holland in beroering. Oproeren in de 17de en 18de eeuw* (1982)
Duke, A. *Reformation and revolt in the Low Countries* (1990)
Fedorowicz, J.K. *A republic of nobles. Studies in Polish history to 1864* (1982)
Fletcher, A. *Tudor rebellions* (1968)
Fletcher, A. en J. Stevenson eds. *Order and disorder in early modern England* (1985)
Gambrelle, F. en M. *Trebitsch eds. Révolte et société. Actes du colloque d'histoire au présent, Paris mai 1968* (1989) 2 vols
Garlan, Y. en C. Nières *Les révoltes bretonnes de 1675. Papier timbré et bonnets rouges* (1975)
Goldstone J.A. *Revolution and rebellion in the early modern world* (1991)
Heller, H. *Iron and blood. Civil wars in sixteenth-century France* (1991)
Knecht, R.J. *The French wars of religion 1559-1598* (1989)
Le Goff, J. en J.-C. Schmitt eds. *Le Charivari* (1981)
Magagna, V.V. *Communities of grain. Rural rebellion in comparative perspective* (1991)
Manning R.B. *Village revolts. Social protest and popular disturbances in England 1509-1640* (1988)
Nicolas, J. ed. *Mouvements populaires et conscience social, XVIe-XIXe siècles* (1985)
Russell, C.S.R. 'Monarchies, wars and estates in England, France and Spain, c.1580-c.1640' in: *Legislative Studies Quarterly 7* (1982)
Scott, T. en B. Schribner *The German peasants' war. A history in documents* (1991)
Tilly, C. *Contentious French* (1986)
Tilly, C. *European revolutions, 1492-1992* (1993)
Trossbach, W. *Soziale Bewegung und politische Erfahrung. Bäuerliche Protest in hessischen Territorien 1648-1806* (1987)
Underdown, D. *Revel, riot and rebellion. Popular politics and culture in England 1603-1660* (1985)
Wong, B. 'Les émeutes de subsistances en Chine et en Europe Occidentale' in: *Annales; economies, sociétés, civilisations 38* (1983)
Zagorin, P. *Rebels and rulers, 1550-1660* (1982) 2 vols

Offstage in the wings
Acerra, M. 'Rochefort: reve et réalité' in: *Neptunia 47* (1982)
Coad, J.G. *The royal dockyards 1690-1850. Architecture and engineering works of the sailing navy* (1989)
Cros, B. 'Les ingénieurs de la marine aux XVIIe et XVIIIe siècles' in: *Neptunia 170* (1988)
Harris, D.G. F.H. Chapman. *The first naval architect and his work* (1989)
Howard, F. *Sailing ships of war 1400-1860* (1990)

Lombaerde, P. 'Maritieme arsenaalssteden tussen 1750 en 1850' in: *de Physieke Existentie dezes Lands. Jan Blanken, inspecteur van de waterstaat (1755-1838)* (1987)
Meer, Sj. de *'s Lands Zeemagazijn* (1992)
Marzari, M. *Progretti per l'imperatore: Andrea Salvini ingegnere a l'arsenal 1802-1817* (1990)
Wiel, A. *The navy of Venice* (1910)

The Spanish civil war
Aróstegui, J. en J. Martínez *La Junta de Defensa de Madrid* (1984)
Bolloten, B. *La guerra civil española* (1989)
Carr, R. *The Spanish tragedy: the Civil War in perspective* (1977)
Fraser, R. *Recuérdalo tú y recuérdalo a otros. Historia oral de la guerra civil española* (1979)
Jackson, G. *The Spanish Republic and the Civil War 1931-1939* (1965)
Salas Larrazabal, R. en J.M. Salas Larrazabal *Historia general de la guerra de España* (1985)
Thomas, H. *The Spanish Civil War* (1977)
Tuñón de Lara, M. ed. *La guerra civil española: 50 años después* (19850
Viñas, V. *La Alemania nazi y el 18 de julio* (1977)
Zugazagoitia, Z. *Historia de la guerra de España* (1940)

The front soldier
Bartov, O. *The Eastern front 1941-1945: German troops and the barbarisation of warfare* (1982)
Baynes, J. *Morale: a study of men and courage* (1967)
Ellis, J. *The sharp end of war* (1980)
Gray, J.G. *The warriors: reflections on men in battle* (1970)
Griffith, P. *Forward to battle* (1981)
Holmes, R. *Firing line* (1985)
Keegan, J. *The face of battle* (1976)
Kellett, A. *Combat motivation* (1982)
Moran, L. *The anatomy of courage* (1966)
Richardson, F.M. *Fighting spirit* (1978)

Mass armies
Aron, R. *Paix et guerre entre nations* (1962)
Bertaud, J.-P. en D. Reichel *Atlas de la Révolution Française vol. 3 L'armée et la guerre* (1989)
Bernard, H. *Guerre totale et guerre révolutionaire 3 vols.* (1965)
Calvocoressi, P. *World politics since 1945* (1987)
Chailiand, G. *Anthologie mondiale de la stratégie, des origines au nucléaire* (1990)
Vos, L. de *Les 4 jours de Waterloo, 15-16-17-18 Juin 1815* (1990)
Dupuy, R.E. en T.N. Dupuy *The encyclopedia of military history, from 3500 B.C. to the present* (1986)
Taylor, A.J.P. *How wars begin* (1980)

ILLUSTRATIONS

144